(Not) Just

Another

Ballgame

Stories from Baseball's

Past

By Kevin Trusty

Foreword by Gary Livacari

TABLE OF CONTENTS

Acknowledgements

Much thanks and appreciation is due to the following folks, without whom this book would not be possible.

To my family, for your endless support and, as baseball fans yourselves, encouraging me as a wee lad to play and learn the game, and then to write about it all these years later.

To Gary, for helping with this book and allowing me an outlet over the years to publish many of my historical baseball essays.

To Denise and Rebekah, for all your expertise, assistance and flexibility with editing and publishing another labor of love project.

To Molly, for once again creating amazing art that captures the vibe of all things.

To Todd, for your crucial creative assistance.

To fellow SABR members for your tireless and passionate research and writings about the history of the game. Your resourcefulness and assistance cannot be measured.

And to you, the baseball fan.

Foreword

by Gary Livacari

Kevin Trusty and I have had an interesting working relationship over the past few years.

He had been an occasional guest contributor to my website, *Baseball History Comes Alive*, and what started as a professional correspondence soon grew into a friendship, due to some of our shared interests: Our love of the Chicago Cubs, our Illinois upbringing, and our enjoyment of reading and writing about baseball history, especially the Deadball Era.

Early on, I discovered Kevin possessed a well-developed appreciation for baseball's glorious past which he always reflected in his writing. This is often hard to find among younger generations of fans.

Whenever Kevin sent me an essay, he never failed to come through with one that was well written, well researched, provocative, and quite often just a bit off the beaten path. Over time, I saw Kevin mature as a writer, and after reading these selections for his new book, *(Not) Just Another Ballgame: Stories from Baseball's Past,* he's now emerged, in my estimation, as one of the most talented young baseball essayists on the American scene today.

When Kevin asked me to write the foreword to his new book, I quickly informed him that I'd be happy to do so. After all, as I told him, "we're kindred spirits." We've never been ones to accept baseball's conventional wisdom. We're skeptics in a way, not always satisfied with superficial explanations.

And we're not afraid to ask tough, thought-provoking questions.

This inherent skepticism was never more apparent than in our shared view of the 1919 Black Sox scandal. Until I met Kevin, I often thought I was the only person on earth who felt there was a lot more to this sordid story waiting to be uncovered and told. I knew I had found a fellow traveler in Kevin. We both found the conventional *Eight Men*

Out version of events to be unsatisfying. The basis for our shared skepticism is a story for another day but suffice it to say we both felt there was a lot more here than met the eye. This excerpt from Kevin's essay, *The 1919 World Series: Did the White Sox Lose, or Did the Reds Win?"* will give you an idea:

What makes deciphering the scandal such a mess (a century later or not), was that it was a mess in itself at the time.

Nobody will ever know the real truth because even the players themselves didn't fully know – or didn't want to know – what was going on. The Reds heard the rumors but shooed them off, and instead focused on winning games. For the White Sox, it was always unclear, even among the team, who was really trying to win and who wasn't, and who may have been double-crossing who.

Imagine being in that clubhouse with all the uncertainty!

Those doubts alone would presumably cast major mental anguish on a ballplayer. How could they look their teammates in the eye? What could they say without sounding paranoid at best or like an untrusting rat at worst? Not to mention the constant barrage of questions from teammates, manager Kid Gleason, owner Charles Comiskey, reporters, and fans, which must have added to the distractions and intrateam discontent.

All of this likely impaired the White Sox's ability to be mentally ready to play in the series. Sure, they managed to deal with their personal differences throughout the season and reach the World Series, but the discord was reaching critical mass by this point.

Individually, the "Clean Sox" players, plus guys like Jackson and Weaver – who were in on discussions of the fix, but their excellent play and stout denials of actual involvement indicated they were trying to win – must have gone through hell trying to play while unsure of their teammates' real intentions.

Now that's provocative!

And it's also a nice sampling of what you can expect from this new collection of Kevin's essays. You won't necessarily find conventional views or conventional writing here. Kevin's a free-thinker who's not afraid to stir things up. Combine that approach with his engaging—and often quirky—writing style, and the fresh perspective he brings to historical events, and I can guarantee you it'll make for entertaining baseball reading.

The essays cover some big, if overlooked events in baseball's history, from the early days of the Dead Ball Era with *Mathewson's Monumental Marvel of 1905* to a special chapter about modern baseball and the Cubs' 2016 World Series championship. Along the way there are many entertaining stops, including the 1920's with *A Lucky Bounce or Three: Washington's Wild 1924 World Series Win*, and the 1940's with *The AAGBBL Turns on the Lights at Wrigley Field*. And if you don't think Kevin has the courage to reexamine events from the past, you will after you read, *Ruth's*

Mysterious Gambit: The Final Out of the 1926 World Series.

Previous, condensed versions of the selected essays have appeared with many others over the years on Kevin's popular blog, *Radbourn's Revenant.* These are some of his best works.

If you enjoy reading about baseball's past and having a little thought-provoking fun, you can't do better than this book that's in your hands. You won't be disappointed.

-Gary Livacari

Pre-game

The Starting Lineup

The Starting Lineup

~ * ~

Baseball.

The very name of the game tends to invoke memories and stories of your favorite players and teams, but it can also touch on some sentimentality for the past; a feeling of nostalgia that casual fans ignore, and purists hold dear.

When you dive even deeper into America's pastime, however, you'll find that the essence of baseball is about many other things.

It is a spiritual and superstitious game.

It is a sport in which players' performances are constantly and continually gauged against their ghostly counterparts from years – even centuries – past. Some ballparks are reportedly haunted. When you watch a game, even with all the modern attributes abound, it still *feels* old. It also feels

14

connective, even enchanted, as though some sense of a *something* might be behind it all. The game's sayings and spiritisms reach far beyond the diamond, pervading into our everyday lives. This includes popular culture as well, with many stories of ethereal, and even hellish baseball afterlives living on in books, films, theater, and music.

How often do you hear, or even say yourself, that something "came out of left field," or was "knocked out of the park?" How many "ballpark figures" have you given or asked for when trying to ascertain a number? These and other baseball idioms are boundless.

The game has a rich history filled with treasurable icons, not the least of which include all the long-gone ballparks.

These fields of old were a far cry from the luxurious and cavernous venues of today. Once upon a time, ballparks were *ballparks*: Cramped, dingy structures encircling a field where the players performed their feats of grace. Live marching bands entertained the crowd in the grandstands before the game and in-between innings. The fans dressed to the nines, with the ladies in their best dresses and the men in tailored suits. Cigar smoke filled the air. The shadier types whispered tricky dealings to each other, hiding their eyes under the brims of their Fedoras so as not to betray their ulterior motives.

Each old ballpark was its own unique, dramatic world. Sadly, only the likes of Fenway Park and Wrigley Field (and to another extent, Dodger Stadium) remain of the old style now. But even all those have undergone massive renovations over the years while adding modern amenities.

It's a game of coincidences, perhaps more than any other sport.

Baseball encompasses a vast quantity of mere *chance* and the randomness that results from it. Sometimes, that random chance permeates into parts of fandom, almost becoming tangible. Like when I attended a game between the Chicago Cubs and Philadelphia Phillies at Wrigley Field on July 25,

2015. I'd been to countless Cubs games over the years, but something just felt a tad different, for whatever reason, before this game. Perhaps I was just appreciating the unique Friday afternoon atmosphere in Wrigleyville more on this day than others, or maybe it was all the delicious Old Styles. Probably both, but I still felt compelled to embrace this particular day more than usual.

So, while waiting in the security line at the main gate underneath the famous Wrigley Field marquee sign, my friend Bill and I both decided to keep a scorecard for the first time since we were kids. Just for the hell of it. We bought the $2 scorecards from the vendor just inside the entrance, not thinking much else of it. We are both glad we did because Phillies' pitcher Cole Hamels proceeded to throw a no-hitter. Yes, I still have the scorecard and the pencil that came with it.

It was amazing to witness a slice of baseball history.

Somewhat ironically, Hamels wound up pitching for the Cubs three years later.

Speaking of the players, they're the ones who truly make the game what it is. Whether a revered hero or an unknown roster filler, every player contributes to the ongoing saga of America's pastime in ways that can be exaggerated or unappreciated, or any point in-between.

Baseball players themselves are somewhat paradoxical by nature. At once they are graceful and clumsy; strong and sensitive; calculating and impulsive; heroic and tragic. But from those qualities come stories, and the great ones beget folklore.

Take Rogers Hornsby, as but one of countless examples. Here was a spectacular ballplayer, arguably the greatest right-handed hitter of all time, who passed into legend with his share of folklore about him and his career milestones. As one tale goes, a rookie pitcher was facing Hornsby, and threw him three pitches, all called balls. Frustrated over the 3-0 count, he argued with famous longtime umpire Bill Klem that all three pitches were strikes. Klem allegedly removed his mask and said "Son, when you pitch a strike, Mr. Hornsby will let you know." [1]

Add all that up and you'll find that in essence, the heart of baseball is awe-inspiring, impressive, and...pretty damn weird.

~ * ~

That brings us to this book.

Since the game's conception, the art of storytelling in baseball has had one common thread: It tends to be exaggerative. For better or worse, there is just something about baseball that welcomes embellished viewpoints to enhance its already surreal experience.

---

[1] https://bleacherreport.com/articles/1368021-nlds-game-4-umpire-jim-joyce-takes-bat-out-of-cardinals-hands

The stories in this book are no exception, and that's the fun of it all.

The intent of this essay collection is to be an acknowledgement and appreciation of some of that surrealism; an infatuation with the history, nuances, and lucky bounces that only baseball, by its mythologized nature, can provide.

I've posted variants of many of these essays over the years on my blog, radbournsrevenant.com. The site's name is a nod to the ghost of one of the game's all-time great pitchers, Charles "Old Hoss" Radbourn, a winner of 60* games in 1884, among many other career accolades. His exploits may not be mentioned much in *this* book, but he is doubtless one such player from the old days whose now-folkloric aura still draws comparisons over 120 years after his death – and still will 120 years from now.

Each chapter has undergone updates and revision from their original forms with extra anecdotes peppered in for good measure, and maybe a laugh or two.

Admittedly, I inject some of my own thoughts and theories into many of the narratives, but that's another part of what makes writing about baseball fun – it can be engaging and subjective.

Whatever you get out of this book, I hope it at least helps you appreciate some of the goofy and fascinating history of the game just a tick more.

~ * ~

For me, it's a little more than just the numbers.

My love of baseball began in earnest at the age of four. I knew what baseball was by then of course, but it wasn't until the first day of preschool where I began to learn just how fun it could be to experience it firsthand.

My preschool classroom was of the typical sort, at least in how I imagined most preschools were in those days: A large, orange-carpeted rectangle surrounded by shelves and nooks of various sizes, all brimming with books, art supplies, and toys.

Early on that first day, I noticed one such toy perilously clinging to the edge of a shelf under a window, as if beckoning me to rescue it from certain fall. Perched between Mr. Potato Head and a stack of board games was a pair of thin, cloth gloves shaped like baseball mitts. The gloves contained a wiffleball lined on all sites with Velcro strips – the idea being it'd be impossible to not catch the ball as long as it hit your glove.

As if on cue, a fellow classmate, Matt, (with whom I still laugh about this story to this day,) and I darted over to confiscate this ball-and-glove set. We pried the gloves apart like a wishbone, shared a laugh, and then, with absolutely no regard for classroom order or teacher instruction, rushed out to the hallway to play catch. We did this a few times during that first week, apparently believing that we were invisible and could just stroll out of the classroom whenever we wanted. Just a couple 4-year-olds giving zero fucks.

Not surprisingly, the cloth mitts disappeared from the shelf pretty quickly, but those times of playing catch in a school hallway caused a spark that would fully ignite later that spring when Matt and I, along with many other friends, played in a Tee-ball league. It was our first full-ish experience with the game. The love of baseball has been here since.

My *fascination* with baseball, on the other hand, didn't develop until many years later, and is still an ongoing discovery.

I feel enamored by the old stories in, and of, the sport. Even in today's game, with its advanced analytics and massive amounts of data, the draw to look above and beyond the science to the narrative is too appealing to resist. Understanding and interpreting statistics to some degree is essentially a requirement for being a fan. But like any other business, the numbers in baseball only tell part of the story.

Studying instances of baseball's past, in addition – or deference – to the hard numerical data, can be a ridiculously fascinating endeavor, and raise many interesting questions. It must've been even more so covering the game in the old days before video and instant replay.

Thanks to today's digital advancements, falling down into an online rabbit hole of baseball's yesteryears is a lot of fun. You never know what fun fact or grapevine connection is waiting to be discovered.

Hunting stories in the old fashioned way with books and microfilm is equally enjoyable. The latter method I really enjoyed in recent years when I compiled a four-part feature series for my local newspaper about different times the Chicago Cubs or Chicago White Sox visited my hometown of Joliet, Illinois to play one of the local teams, going as far back as 1876.

There I'd be, in my local library, piecing together recaps of the games themselves, digging deeply into my town's history to locate the ballparks where the games were played, and working with area historical societies and other researchers to find photographs or other interesting tidbits for use in the articles. It's enjoyable.

So, why these particular stories? I chose them for their interesting, impressive, or odd circumstances. This doesn't even scratch the surface though. There are thousands and thousands of tales like this throughout the game's surly history, and even those in this book have been studied and written about many times before – and will be again. However, there is an affinity I have with this particular content, something that drew me to the downright wackiness contained in each.

Like the game itself – and those cloth mitts I found on the first day of preschool – there's just something about baseball...

- *Charles "Old Hoss" Radbourn was a big league pitcher who is most well-known for winning 59* games in 1884. However, modern research has led to a new interpretation of the records in which Radbourn is now credited with 60 wins that season.*

First Inning

A Lucky Bounce or *Three*: Washington's Wild World Series Win in 1924

First Inning

A Lucky Bounce or *Three*: Washington's Wild World Series Win in 1924

The 1924 World Series can be somewhat dryly summed up this way: Seven games. Four of them decided by one run. Two games went to extra innings.

While on the surface that may sound pretty appetizing as far as excitement, it still feels like something of an understatement when considering how the whole series ended. When all was said and done, the '24 World Series would become an absolute classic.

It was also one of the strangest, too. Particularly the seventh and deciding game.

Famed New York skipper John McGraw led his powerhouse Giants into Griffith Stadium on the 10th of October, hoping to swipe the series from the hometown Washington Senators and secure his third world championship in four years.

However, the Senators' player-manager Bucky Harris, along with his ace pitcher and future Hall of Famer Walter "Big Train" Johnson – and perhaps a bit of divine intervention – had other plans.

The series was a seesaw battle up to this point, with each team winning alternate games. But what seemed odd was that the great Walter Johnson of the Senators had pitched far below his potential and had actually taken the losses in Games 1 and 5. Running out of arms, options and luck, Harris was in need of a little help if his Washington club was going to win their long-sought after championship.

Washington's Curly Ogden started on the hill, but Harris pulled him after facing just two batters and retiring one, as he gave way to George Mogridge. It was theorized, conceivably, that Harris started the righty Ogden so that McGraw would be forced to load his lineup with left-handed hitters, and who would then have to face the lefty Mogridge with virtually no preparation. The ploy seemingly worked, as Mogridge turned in a solid outing over the next

4.2 innings, allowing one earned run and scattering four hits.

A young righty, Firpo Marberry, came on in relief for Mogridge in the sixth, but after two unearned runs swiftly crossed the plate, the Senators found themselves in a 3-1 deficit entering the late innings. Marberry shut down the Giants in the seventh and eighth, but the problems continued with the Senators' bats. The Giants' starting pitcher Virgil Barnes was cruising along, only allowing one run to this point, coming on a Bucky Harris home run in the fourth inning.

With one out in the bottom of the eighth inning, and the overflow D.C. crowd getting anxious, Harris inserted pinch hitter Nemo Liebold, a scrappy outfielder who had previously appeared in both the 1917 and 1919 World Series with the Chicago White Sox.

Liebold promptly roped a double, followed by a single from catcher Muddy Ruel and the Griffith Stadium throng was on the verge of erupting. With

Marberry's job done for the day, Bennie Tate stepped in to pinch-hit. Like any good batsman whose job it is to get on base or at least move the runners in that situation, he drew a walk, which loaded the bases.

Suddenly Barnes' fine effort was coming to a screeching halt.

With the game in the balance, Harris entered the box and got the assistance he sorely needed, when his routine chopper to third baseman Freddie Lindstrom took a wild hop over his head. The fortunate bounce plated two runs and tied the game. The 31,667 in attendance broke into wild cheers as their club found new life late in the deciding contest. The short barrage chased Barnes from the hill after 7 2/3 strong innings.

As it was late in the game and series, Harris had few choices on available pitchers for this situation. In going with his gut, he called upon Johnson to step to the bump in the ninth.

Despite his lackluster performances earlier in the series, The Big Train started to roll from his first pitch and completely shut the Giants down. After failing to score in the bottom of the ninth, Game 7 headed to extras, and Johnson continued to dismantle the Giants' batters through the 10th, 11th, and 12th innings.

It was then, in the bottom of the 12th, when Harris and his Senators got another big break that they needed – this time, perhaps, with a little assistance from the beyond.

With one out in the inning, Giants pitcher Jack Bentley jammed catcher Muddy Ruel, forcing him to loop a soft foul popup behind the plate. The Giants' stout catcher Hank Gowdy hopped, but he unfortunately stumbled over his own dropped mask and was unable to make the play. Ruel was miraculously still alive in the at-bat, facing pressure to reach base. On the very next pitch, he took advantage of his second chance, and drilled a double to left field.

This brought up the pitcher, Walter Johnson. Known as a pretty fair hitter for a pitcher, Johnson managed to rap a sharp grounder down toward third base but just to Lindstrom's left, where he and shortstop Travis Jackson became the victims of yet another bad hop. Neither was able to field the ball cleanly, which put runners on first and second with one out.

Senators center fielder Earl McNeely came up to bat next and the nervous crowd at Griffith Stadium was collectively hoping for a clean hit – or at least one more miraculous bounce – that could score Ruel.

As if by some ethereal orchestration beyond coincidence, McNeely slapped a grounder toward third, where the ball took off on *another* unlucky hop over Lindstrom's head.

The safe hit plated Ruel for the series' winning run.

If the Senators' fans had been praying for a miracle late in the game, they ended up with three.

Like hockey playoffs, baseball has a funny way of having things bounce your way, or against you, a time or two...or three in this case.

After the game, Bentley, credited with the loss, summed up the bizarre afternoon:

"That was one of the strangest games I ever played in. With one out, Hank Gowdy did a sun dance on Ruel's pop foul and stepped into his mask and dropped the ball. Ruel doubled and then there was an error at short, then McNeely hit that grounder. That was a helluva way to lose a World Series." [1]

The 1924 world championship was the first and only title for the Washington Senators.

The D.C. club would win the American League pennant again in 1925 but lose a close battle in the World Series to the Pittsburgh Pirates, four games to three. The Senators reached the World

---

[1] https://bleacherreport.com/articles/1386103-washington-nationals-remembering-the-1924-world-series

Series once more in 1933 but lost to the New York Giants four games to one.

In 1961, the carousel of clubs began when the franchise moved out of D.C. to Minneapolis and became the Minnesota Twins, eventually winning World Series titles in 1987 and 1991. At the same time, an expansion Washington Senators team remained in D.C. until 1972, when they relocated to the far south of Arlington, becoming the Texas Rangers.

Washington D.C. would not field a Major League Baseball team again until 2005, when the Montreal Expos franchise moved there and became the Washington Nationals.

It wouldn't be until 2019 when Washington's ballclub would hoist another World Series trophy.

Nearly 100 years earlier, though, Harris, Johnson, and a few wild bounces ensured that Washington would reach baseball's pinnacle.

'Tis a weird game, folks.

Second Inning

The AAGBBL Turns on the Lights at Wrigley Field

Second Inning

The AAGBBL Turns on the Lights at Wrigley Field

Baseball, as we know, is a strange game of numbers, dates, and bizarre coincidences. There are also plenty of overlooked facts, as well.

9 August 1988

The Chicago Cubs earn a 6-4 victory over the New York Mets in the first official night game at Wrigley Field — except it was supposed to be the second game under the lights at Wrigley. Instead, it became the first official *completed* night game at the friendly confines. Sort of.

8 August 1988

On a blustery and stormy evening, a game between the Cubs and visiting Philadelphia Phillies was finally called midway through the fourth inning after a lengthy rain delay. Mother Nature had other plans for the would-be first official night game at Wrigley Field — only that it was considered the first

37

night game at Wrigley Field wasn't exactly true, though.

The Cubs-Phillies tilt was to be the first MLB night game at Wrigley, but it was not the first *professional* game to grace the ivy in the starlight at Clark & Addison.

For that contest, you'll have to journey all the way back to July 1, 1943.

On that summer night, an All-Star game made up of players from the All-American Girls Base Ball League (AAGBBL) took place. The league was in its first season, still finding their way, and decades before being immortalized in the smash hit 1992 film, *A League of Their Own.*

Official night games in professional baseball began in 1935 at Crosley Field in Cincinnati. On May 24 of that year, the Philadelphia Phillies trained across the Ohio River for a late-spring matchup against the Reds. In a grandiose pregame ceremony "overseen" by President Franklin Delano Roosevelt (he was actually at the White House, not the

ballpark), night baseball was officially underway.[1]
Major League teams began adding lights to their
stadiums over the next several years, including the
Cubs at Wrigley, but the tragic events of December
7, 1941 changed those plans at the ballpark on
Chicago's north side.

The Cubs were slated to host night games
beginning in the 1942 season. But immediately after
the infamous attack on Pearl Harbor, the Cubs
donated all the steel and useful parts of the lights to
the ensuing war effort.

A shortage of material then halted the project
for the duration of World War II. After the war,
much debating over whether to install lights at
Wrigley continued for the next several years. In the
early 1960s, the promise of nighttime baseball
returned, but only if the Cubs became worthy of
possessing the modern feature. By the early 1980s,

1

https://www.cincinnati.com/story/sports/mlb/reds/2020/05/
22/mlb-first-night-baseball-game-crosley-field-1935-reds-
phillies/5195230002/

official legislation actually banned night games at Wrigley Field, a decision that was not overturned until 1988. [2]

Nearly five decades after the AAGBBL All-Star night game, the Cubs finally began hosting night games of their own.

Long before the Cubs' inaugural night gam e however, night baseball did happen at Wrigley Field, courtesy of the AAGBBL, in its original incarnation. The league's name would be changed prior to the 1944 season to its more recognized title as the All-American Girls Professional Baseball League, or AAGPBL.

For this 1943 All-Star occasion, crews placed portable lights behind home plate and down the first and third baselines.

The first season of the AAGBBL included four teams. The games would be played with standard baseball rules but use a 12-inch softball,

---

[2] http://www.chicagology.com/baseball/wrigleylights/

shortened basepaths, and underhand pitching to create a sort of hybrid-style game. The ball size continued to shrink every year, eventually equaling the size of a standard baseball, and overhand pitching was allowed by 1948. With this, the length of the basepaths regularly increased, along with the distance of the pitcher's mound to home plate, finally reaching 60 feet by 1954. [3]

While the first *official* AAGPBL All-Star Game wouldn't occur until 1946, the league's stars assembled on this forgotten July night in '43 for a special contest.

The game nearly fell on the 10-year anniversary of the first MLB All-Star Game, which took place at Chicago's other legendary ball yard, Comiskey Park, in 1933.

The two 1943 AAGBBL All-Star teams were split among the league's participating members. One team consisted of a mixed Illinois-Indiana roster, featuring players from the Rockford Peaches and

---

[3] https://www.aagpbl.org/history/rules-of-play

South Bend Blue Sox. The other was the all-Wisconsin team, made up of members of the Racine Belles and Kenosha Comets.

The game itself was the headline event of the evening, and a one-sided affair at that, as the Wisconsin squad decimated the Illinois-Indiana group by a final tally of 16-0.

It was actually something of a day-night doubleheader.

The daytime opener featured a softball game which was put on by the WAAC (Women's Army Auxiliary Corps). In this game, Fort Sheridan defeated Camp Grant by a score of 11-5.

Researcher Jay Feldman acquired some insightful AAGBBL player feedback on the nighttime contest.

"The lights weren't all that great, but we were used to that — we had to play with whatever we had," said Shirley Jameson of the Kenosha Comets. "Besides, just the fact that we were playing in Wrigley

Field was enough. We'd have done it whether it was light or dark, because we were all on Cloud Nine."[4]

Playing whatever, wherever and with whatever they had was typical in those early days, and even turned into a sort of mantra for the players and coaches. The shared pride among the teams with regard to that very sentiment became something of a rallying point for the league itself during that inaugural season.

This continued as the league expanded very quickly, adding new teams as soon as the following year and continually drawing more and more fans, long after the war years.

The league swiftly became its own spectacle, in some ways due to the success of this first night contest.

---

[4] https://baseballhall.org/discover/1943-aagpbl-all-star-game-played-under-lights-at-wrigley-field

Here is the official box score of the night game:

Box score from the July 1, 1943 AAGBBL All Star Game from the July 2 edition of the Kenosha Evening News, sourced from sabr.org

Center fielder Betsy "Sock 'Em" Jochum of the South Bend Blue Sox went about the game as usual.

"I didn't realize at the time that they didn't have lights at Wrigley Field," she said. "I just thought those lights were there all the time. We showed up for the game, the lights were on, and we played." [5]

The league returned to Wrigley Field a year later for another special contest, once again using portable lights. On July 18, 1944, the now-named AAGPBL played a twi-night doubleheader as a benefit for the Red Cross.

The AAGPBL continued under that name until 1945, when it went back to the AAGBBL at the end of that season, where it remained until 1950. The name was then shortened to the American Girls Baseball League (AGBL), before being restored to the AAGPBL, as it is recognized today. [6]

These overlooked night games in 1943 and 1944 are not only significant in being the first professional night games at Wrigley Field, but are also a small example which further signifies the

---

[5] https://sabr.org/gamesproj/game/july-1-1943-all-american-girls-play-first-game-under-the-lights-at-wrigley-field/ (article also appeared in "Wrigley Field: The Friendly Confines at Clark and Addison, (SABR 2019), edited by Gregory H. Wolf)
[6] https://www.aagpbl.org/history/league-history

remarkable role these women played in wartime, and post-war American culture.

The AAGPBL was absolutely crucial in keeping professional baseball going during the war years and the impact of the league – which operated until 1954 and included over 600 women – created a lasting impact on our nation's baseball history.

Oh, and speaking of those bizarre coincidences, *A League of Their Own* debuted in theaters on July 1, 1992 – which was 49 years later, to the day, of when the AAGBBL became the first professional group to play ball under the lights at Wrigley Field.

Third Inning

The Greatest Game Babe
Ruth Ever Pitched?

Third Inning

The Greatest Game Babe Ruth Ever Pitched?

When it comes to historical references to baseball, or even just casual generalities of the game, Babe Ruth is the name that is mentioned most often. The contexts surrounding him range from common phrases all the way to something of a god-worshipping reverence.

Even to those who don't follow baseball, Ruth is a well-known figure.

In the early years of his Major League career, well before he became the near-mythical Yankees slugger for which he is most renowned, The Babe was a terrific pitcher for the Boston Red Sox. In 1916, he was tops of the World Series champions' staff, compiling a 23-12 record with an American League-leading 1.75 ERA. Along with that, he included 23 complete games while firing 323 innings.

Arguably his pinnacle, if overlooked, performance came on a rather big stage: Game 2 of the 1916 World Series.

In order to accommodate a larger crowd than what could be squeezed into Fenway Park, the game was played at nearby Braves Field, home of Boston's National League club. The Red Sox entered Game 2 with a 1-0 series lead over the Brooklyn Robins (before they became the Dodgers.) Ruth would take the mound against Brooklyn's Sherry Smith, a solid pitcher himself who went 14-10 with a 2.34 ERA on the 1916 season. The battle of southpaws in this game would prove to be pivotal in the series.

It was already an important game, but what eventually transpired on this day was an incredible 14-inning contest that left fans anxiously captivated even as darkness descended on the then-new Boston ballpark.

This game would also certify Ruth as a true ace.

With two outs in the top of the first inning, Brooklyn's Hi Myers launched a ball off Ruth to right center field that got past both Harry Hooper and Tilly Walker. With the two outfielders unable to corral the carom off the wall, Myers chugged all the way around the bases for an inside the park home run.[1]

Neither team scored in the second, but the Red Sox were able to tie it up in the third when Ruth's groundout scored shortstop Everett "Deacon" Scott, who had led off the inning with a triple.

For the next several innings both teams took threatening turns to gain the lead. But gallant pitching by both Ruth and Smith, along with their excellent defenses held serve as neither offense could flash a run across the dish.

With the score still tied 1-1 in the bottom of the ninth, Boston's second baseman Hal Janvrin led off the inning with a double. The next batter, pinch

[1] Cecilia Tan and Bill Nowlin, *Braves Field: Memorable Moments at Boston's Lost Diamond.*

hitter Jimmy Walsh, reached on an error, advancing Janvrin to third. Just like that, the Red Sox had something cooking with runners at the corners and nobody out.

First baseman Dick Hoblitzell stepped in and lofted a fly ball to center field. This brought the crowd to their feet with the promise that the airborne horsehide would be the game-winning sacrifice fly. Brooklyn center fielder Hi Myers, contributing on both sides for his Robins, camped under the ball, ready to make a desperation toss to try and nab Janvrin. He retired Hoblitzell's fly, then came up firing a rocket to home, pegging Janvrin at the plate and preserving the tie. Smith intentionally walked Duffy Lewis next to get to Larry Gardner, who would foul out to end the inning. The game was headed to extras.[2]

As was the case all game long, both teams threatened runs in each of the first couple extra innings but couldn't capitalize. Since there were no

---

[2] Tan, Nowlin

lights at the ballpark (regular Major League night games wouldn't occur for another 19 years), time was becoming the most crucial factor. Daylight was quickly fading, and the game would be ruled a tie if they couldn't finish one way or another soon.

Brooklyn, trying to seize another opportunity, had their last best chance in the top of the 13th.

With a runner on second and no outs, Sherry Smith, who was still pitching for Brooklyn, looped a Texas leaguer toward left field. Duffy Lewis, an outstanding defensive player in his own right, took a page from the Tris Speaker handbook when he tore in from deep left to make a sensational catch, saving a run and perhaps, the game.

Smith set Boston down in order in the bottom of the 13th, and Ruth followed suit with the Brooklyn hitters in the 14th. The ongoing deadlock combined with encroaching darkness meant it was time for some strategic Deadball Era smallball by the Red Sox.

Hoblitzell did his job masterfully when he led off the bottom of the 14th with a walk – one of four he had on the day. Lewis promptly sacrificed him over to second. Red Sox skipper Bill Carrigan inserted the speedy Mike McNally to pinch run for Hoblitzell, and at the same time, called upon Del Gainer to pinch-hit for the struggling Larry Gardner.

The switches worked like a charm.

Gainer roped a single to left field and McNally, with no hesitation rounding third, beat a strong throw by future Hall of Fame outfielder Zack Wheat to the plate. The standing-room crowd erupted, as the run gave Boston a 2-1 victory and a two-game lead in the series.

The brilliantly executed 14th-frame heroics catapulted the Red Sox on to win the series in five games, securing their second consecutive World Championship.

Not lost amid the thrilling finale to this game was the incredible pitching by both Sherry Smith and the victorious Babe Ruth, who both went the distance.

Smith's final line tallied 13.1 innings, scattering seven hits and two earned runs while walking six and striking out two. Ruth was even better, going the full 14 innings, allowing only six hits and one run, with four strikeouts and three free passes. He also had a key RBI in the third inning that tied the game at 1 before the victors broke the long stalemate.

The Game 2 win not only put the Red Sox in the driver's seat to clinch the series, but it solidified Ruth as a big-game pitcher who really put an exclamation point on his terrific regular season.

Two years later, Ruth would twirl another gem in the World Series, shutting out the Chicago Cubs 1-0 in the opening game. As impressive as that was, his Game 2 sensation against Brooklyn in 1916 may have been better.

Ruth would enjoy a couple more productive seasons on the mound for the Red Sox, but by 1918 his powerful bat really began to emerge, and 1919 saw him achieve true slugger status. Prior to the 1920 season he was sold to the New York Yankees, where he helped them create a dynasty and while launching himself into legendary status thereafter.

Yet long before having his likeness carved into the Mount Rushmore of baseball legends, the stocky, hot dog-loving kid from Baltimore was quite the sensational southpaw on the hill.

Fourth Inning

The Brakeman Completes
Another One

Fourth Inning

The Brakeman Completes Another One

One of the common, if also understated, superlatives bestowed upon many early Deadball Era pitchers is that they were indestructible.

More specifically, that their *arms* were.

A token glance at the pitching stats of late 19th and early 20th century legends like Cy Young, Pud Galvin, Old Hoss Radbourn, and Cannonball Crane among others, reveal some hysterical (by modern standards) numbers in terms of games started, games completed, and innings pitched.

With the completed games category in mind, one such dapper gent of the mound achieved a rather asinine feat that the rest did not: He threw 187 *consecutive* complete games.

Jack Taylor began his pro career in 1897 with the Milwaukee Brewers of the old Western League, a team managed by the legendary future Hall of

Fame skipper, Connie Mack. He wouldn't stay in the Western League long, as he broke into the big leagues when the Chicago Orphans (before they were the Cubs) purchased his contract late in the 1898 season. He would remain there through 1903.

On June 20, 1901, Taylor took the loss in a complete-game performance against the Boston Beaneaters (before they became the Braves) at the South End Grounds. Nobody anticipated that this game would be the start of Taylor's remarkable feat, wherein he completed every game he started for the next four-plus seasons.

Nicknamed "Brakeman Jack" in reference to his railroad occupation in the offseason, Taylor was a non-flashy, tough-as-nails righthander from New Straitsville, Ohio. His breakout season came in 1902 where he compiled a 23-11 mark with a sizzling 1.29 ERA, along with 34 complete games in 34 starts. That season, he was the league leader in ERA, WHIP (0.953) and shutouts (8.)

After the 1902 regular season ended, the Cubs and their crosstown rival White Sox engaged in an exhibition "City Series", something that would become a Chicago tradition for many years to come. In this particular series, Taylor was accused of throwing a game to the White Sox. Though nothing was ever officially proven, he was nonetheless traded during the winter of 1903 to the St. Louis Cardinals. [1]

This trade would end up holding some fame of its own.

Taylor was part of a deal along with catcher/first baseman Larry McLean for catcher Jack O'Neill and a young, unproven, and undervalued pitcher named Mordecai Brown. At the time, it seemed the Cardinals got the better half of the deal, but not long afterward that table turned as Mordecai "Three Finger" Brown would go on to win two World Series' (appearing in four), with the Cubs and lock his own valued place in baseball's Hall of Fame.

---

[1] http://charlesapril.com/2009/08/closer-look-jack-taylors-complete-game.html

Meanwhile, Brakeman Jack's complete game streak continued with the Cardinals, as he sealed up 39 of them to lead the league, along with 20 victories in 1904. Amid repeated accusations of throwing games – which was common rumbling in those days – and none of which were proven, Taylor became a fairly mixed commodity. On July 1, 1906 he was traded back to the Cubs, and the timing couldn't have been better.

Once he returned to Chicago, Taylor joined an outstanding and now-famous championship pitching staff led by Brown, along with Orval Overall, Carl Lundgren, Jack Pfiester, and Ed Reulbach.

The Brakeman picked up in Chicago where he'd left off in St. Louis, completing his first nine starts. Finally, on August 13, he was pulled after just 2.1 innings in a drubbing by the Brooklyn Superbas.

He bounced right back, however, completing his final seven starts, including two shutouts. He added in his own 12-3 mark with the Cubs in the second half of the 1906 season but ended his complete game streak at an astronomical 187. [2]

His combined ERA in 1906 sat at 1.99 (including 1.83 with the Cubs) and was a factor in the Cubs' team ERA, which totaled an unheard of mark of 1.76 for the season. The Cubs would reach the World Series, but ironically fall to the crosstown White Sox, where the famed "Hitless Wonders" of the south side did just enough damage to the elite Cubs pitching staff to take the title.

A year later, Taylor helped the Cubs get back to the World Series, this time emerging as world champs after sweeping the Detroit Tigers in the fall classic. (Although Game 1 actually ended in a 12-inning tie.[3]) 1907 would be Taylor's final big league season, though he would bounce around in the minor leagues for several more years before finally hanging up his professional cleats in 1913.

---

[2] https://www.baseball-reference.com/players/gl.fcgi?id=tayloja02&t=p&year=1906
[3] https://www.baseball-reference.com/postseason/1907_WS.shtml

Taylor returned to Ohio, worked as a miner, and died there in 1938.

For his career, Jack Taylor amassed a 152-139 record, to go along with a career ERA of 2.65. Numbers like that are certainly strong by themselves. But when you consider that he threw 2,626 innings with 20 shutouts while completing 279 games in 287 starts, it's hard not to consider Taylor among the elite, if certainly overlooked hurlers of the early Deadball Era.

The most impressive mark in Taylor's career of course, is his MLB-record of 187 consecutive complete games. That is absolutely crazy to conceive, in any era of baseball, and a mark that will never be touched.

Fifth Inning

A Perfect Game, Perfected?

Fifth Inning

A Perfect Game, Perfected?

Pitching, by its very nature, is controlled chaos.

Great pitching takes that chaos and molds it into an art form within the art of the game. Perfect pitching is even more extraordinary.

To date, there have been just 23 perfect games thrown in more than 150 years of Major League baseball, and well over 200,000 games played.

The feat is equally as rare as it is incredible. But has there ever been such a thing as a *perfect*-perfect game? Addie Joss of the Cleveland Naps may have given us the answer over a century ago.

Some historians consider the 1908 season one of, if not the greatest in the history of baseball for its closely contested, down-to-the-wire pennant races in both leagues, the famous "Merkle Game" in

New York becoming among the most controversial in baseball history, and on a sad note, even a couple riots and deaths. [1]

Packed in the midst of the wild stretch run that season was a key game on October 2 between the Cleveland Naps (Indians) and the Chicago White Sox. Both clubs were neck and neck in the race with the Detroit Tigers, playing a tight game of leapfrog for the American League pennant. It was a must-win contest for both teams and the 10,598 fans [2] at League Park in Cleveland expected to see a good game between future Hall of Fame pitchers Addie Joss and Ed Walsh.

What they got however, was one of the greatest pitching duels of all time.

"So grandly contested were both pennant races, so great the excitement, so tense the interest, that in the last month of the season the entire nation became

---

[1] Cait Murphy, *Crazy '08: How a Cast of Cranks, Rogues, Boneheads, and Magnates Created the Greatest Year in Baseball History*

[2] http://www.baseball-almanac.com/boxscore/10021908.shtml

absorbed in the thrilling and nerve-racking struggle, and even the Presidential campaign was almost completely overshadowed." [3]

– *Sporting Life*, October 17, 1908, p. 3

"Big Ed" Walsh was on fire this game for the White Sox. In fact, he was utterly brilliant, going the distance and allowing just one unearned run on only four hits while striking out 15 Cleveland hitters.

Addie Joss, an extremely likable fellow by all accounts was, amazingly, *better* than Walsh in this game.

He used his unique corkscrew-style windup to unleash blazing fastballs which cut down the pale-hosed hitters like newly mown grass. The White Sox offense stumbled out of the gate and never found any momentum. In fact, they were hardly touching the ball.

3

https://digital.la84.org/digital/collection/p17103coll17/id/3210 8

It wasn't until after the sixth inning when the gravity of the situation finally dawned on the fans: No White Sox player had yet reached base.

Joss' teammates on the Naps (as they were nicknamed then in honor of their star player-manager Napoleon Lajoie), began to avoid him in the dugout between innings, a tradition that carries on to this day during any no-hitter in progress. The crowd at League Park indulged in their own superstition as well, and the final innings were viewed in near silence, a scene that must have been truly strange – even eerie – to witness.

"A mouse working his way along the grandstand floor would have sounded like a shovel scraping over concrete," wrote one reporter. [4]

Down 1-0 in the top of the ninth and desperate to score a run, the White Sox turned to their bench.

---

[4] Murphy

As he had done all day, Joss retired the first two batters quickly.

Now with two outs, White Sox veteran "Honest John" Anderson, a strong, lifetime .290 hitter stepped to the plate. If League Park could have been quieter than silence at that moment, it probably was.

With the first two pitches, Joss put Anderson down in the count 0-2. On the potential strikeout delivery, Anderson rapped a grounder to third, where Bill Bradley, almost too casually, tossed it to George Stovall at first. Stovall played the weak throw well, digging the ball from the dirt in a nice play, but the ball popped up out of his mitt before he could fully secure it.

With Anderson just a step away from the bag, Stovall was able to grab the ball in the nick of time for the 27th and final out of the game.

It was right then that League Park, its collective lips having been sealed in a reverent, church-like fashion for the past couple innings, finally erupted. On a huge day where a win kept the Naps in the pennant race and virtually eliminated the White Sox from contention, one of the best pitching contests of all time ensued, and the home team emerged victorious.

Joss rose to a new height that day, throwing the-then fourth perfect game in big league history and possibly the *most* perfect game of all time. Not only were the game's circumstances massive, but Joss' efficiency was remarkable – he only threw 74 pitches.

With the American League pennant in sight, the Naps would race the Detroit Tigers to the bitter end, with the Tigers squeaking past by just a half game to capture the flag. Detroit went on to face the mighty Chicago Cubs in the World Series, losing four games to one.

Joss finished the 1908 season with an excellent 24-11 mark and a blistering ERA of 1.16. He would win 14 more games the following season and only make a handful of starts in 1910 while battling several injuries. One of those starts was another no-hitter against the White Sox, also by a score of 1-0.

The following spring, Joss fell ill and struggled to improve. By the time he was diagnosed with tuberculosis, the disease had set on too far and reached his brain. Addie Joss died April 14, 1911 at the age of 31.

For his all-too-short nine-year career, young Addie racked up a record of 160-97, with 234 complete games and 45 shutouts. He threw two no-hitters including his 1908 perfect game and compiled a lifetime ERA of just 1.89 which is second all-time only to, ironically, Ed Walsh.

His career WHIP of 0.968 is currently the lowest in MLB history.

In a short but stellar tenure, Addie Joss earned much respect from teammates, fans, and competitors alike.

On this one day in October 1908, he not only delivered at a time his team needed it most, but in doing so he turned in perhaps the most perfectly efficient perfect game that baseball will ever see.

Sixth Inning

The Clowning of Germany Schaefer

Sixth Inning

The Clowning of Germany Schaefer

To say that 1876 was a big year in America might be an understatement.

Our nation celebrated the 100th anniversary of the signing of the Declaration of Independence, and the Centennial Exposition, which was in many ways the first World's Fair, went on in Philadelphia, drawing as many as 10,000,000 estimated visitors [1]

It was a pretty big year in Major League Baseball as well, with the official forming of the National League.

That same year in Chicago, a lad named Herman "Germany" Schaefer was born to German immigrant parents.

Growing up on the city's working class south side, Schaefer was drawn to baseball at a young age,

---

and, by the time he was 18, his impressive defensive skills began to draw the attention of pro scouts. After a couple stints in semi-pro ball, Schaefer moved up through the old Western League, and eventually made his Major League debut in 1901 with the Chicago Cubs.

He would go on to become a valued player throughout his 15-year MLB career.

His big league tenure included time with the Cubs, Detroit Tigers (where he played an important role on two World Series runner-up teams in 1907 and 1908), and the Washington Senators. He jumped to the Federal League's Newark Peppers for the 1915 season, where he was teammates with future Hall of Famers Edd Rousch and Bill McKechnie. Schaefer returned to the American League in 1916 and had a one-game appearance as a member of the New York Yankees. He completed his pro career in 1918 with another one-game showing at the age of 42 with the Cleveland Indians.

Throughout his playing days, he was renowned for being a defensive star, possessing great range and hands that complemented a sharp baseball mind and brilliant sense of timing.

He was also reputed to be a master of deception and wit, including attempting such wizardry as the hidden ball trick, which he employed in a game during the 1907 World Series. [2]

It wasn't just his solid play on the field that earned him notoriety in the big leagues, however; it was his antics. Put another way, Germany "The Prince" Schaefer was a total clown.

Some of his more appreciated comedic highlights in his career include:

- Wearing a raincoat and galoshes to the plate during a drizzly game.
- Hiding out of sight and scaring a drunken umpire at a bar by pretending to be the Voice of God - only to be ejected from a game later

---

[2] https://sabr.org/bioproj/person/2594238c

by that same umpire when he fessed up to the prank.

- Sporting a fake mustache to the plate, possibly in an attempt to re-enter a game pretending to be another player.

- Homering off a fellow jester, Rube Waddell, only to carry his bat around the bases as if a rifle and pretend to "shoot" the pitcher repeatedly, with both men laughing at the skit.

- Changing his nickname from "Germany" to "Liberty" at the start of World War I.

-

Additionally, Schaefer was an adept trash-talker and sign-taker. But perhaps his two greatest comical feats were his called shot off Doc White in Chicago in 1906, and his stealing of *first* base in 1911.

On June 24, 1906, Schaefer and his Tigers were in Chicago to play the White Sox. Detroit was down 2-1 in the top of the ninth with a man on first and two outs. Detroit skipper Bill Armour inserted Schaefer to pinch-hit for pitcher Red Donahue. After storming back to the dugout, upset that he'd been taken out, Donahue watched hopelessly as salt was poured into his wound by the stunt Schaefer was about to pull.

What happened next is best, (if perhaps highly exaggerated), accounted for by Tigers outfielder Davy Jones, in his quote from Lawrence Ritter's *The Glory of Their Times*:

"Just as he was about to get into the batter's box, he removed his cap and faced the grandstand, bellowing "Ladies and gentlemen, you are now looking at Herman Schaefer, better known as Herman the Great, acknowledged by one and all to be the greatest pinch hitter in the world. I am now going to hit the ball into the left field bleachers. Thank you." [3]

Much to the dismay of the incredulous Chicago crowd at South Side Park, Schaefer blasted the second pitch from Doc White into the left field seats – just like he said he would.

---

[3] Lawrence Ritter, *The Glory of Their Times pp.35-36*

He stood there in gloat, watching the ball in flight, and, after it left the yard, he sprinted to first base where he slid headfirst into the bag. He then leaped up, yelling "Schaefer leads at the Quarter!" Then he took off and slid into second and yelled "Schaefer leads at the Half!" as if he were a prized racehorse on the track. He did the same thing at third and finally home plate, where he got up and declared "Schaefer wins by a nose!" He walked over to the grandstand again in true showboat fashion, saying "Ladies and gentlemen, I thank you for your kind attention." Chaos ensued in the Tigers dugout, where every player was roaring with laughter – except Donahue. [4]

As quite possibly the only one able to outdo him, Schaefer took it upon himself to launch another comedic gem in 1911, also against the White Sox. Only this one was so profound that it would prompt a rule change.

---

[4] Ritter

He stole *first* base.

Schaefer, then playing for the Washington Senators, had one of the best seasons of his career in 1911. The 35-year old hit .334 with an .809 OPS in 125 games. But on August 4th of that year, he would make a play that changed the game of baseball.

It was the bottom of the ninth in a scoreless tie at Griffith Stadium in Washington, D.C. Clyde Milan was on third, with Schaefer on first. He broke on the pitch for second, in an attempt to draw a throw to free up Milan to sprint for home. Fred Payne, the White Sox catcher, didn't take the bait, allowing Schaefer to safely advance. Now it was a second and third situation, and nobody could've guessed what stunt The Prince was about to pull.

On the next pitch, Schaefer led off in the *other* direction and headed back toward first. He swiped the bag back, which must have drawn confused looks from everyone.

Hugh Duffy, managing the White Sox, came out of the dugout to debate Schaefer's bewildering move with the umpire. Meanwhile, Schaefer, believing for whatever reason that play hadn't been officially stopped, took off for second again, while the White Sox defenders scrambled out of their momentary shock. This time, he successfully incited the rundown for Milan that he originally wanted. Milan was thrown out at the plate, however, so the plan backfired. But in typical Schaefer-esque fashion, he and his teammates actually tried to argue that it should've been a dead ball ruling since the White Sox had 10 men on the field when Duffy came out to protest the play. [5]

In the end, the Senators would win 1-0 in extra innings.

Before Schaefer's attempted trickery that day, nobody imagined any logical scenario where a baserunner would want to revert back to the base he came from. Needless to say, Major League Baseball didn't either, so they introduced the rule that you

---

[5] Sabr.org

could *not* steal back a previous base once you advanced past it.

Even with all his silliness and profound goofery, Schaefer had a remarkable and storied career.

He played in 1,150 games through parts of 15 seasons. His career statistics were a bit pedestrian (lifetime .257 hitter with an OPS of .639), but he provided immense worth to each team he played on. Not only for his versatility, defensive prowess and quick-thinking, but for the immeasurable intangibles he brought in the forms of humor, cleverness, and a sense of fun.

Baseball could use more personalities like his.

Seventh Inning

The Mays Malaise

Seventh Inning

The Mays Malaise

Coincidences happen. Though on occasion, and with the biased aid of hindsight, some situations seemingly foretell what's to come.

Baseball analysts and sabermetricians have long been on the hunt for the Holy Grail metric; that figure which can predict what a player will, or at least will be very likely to do. When it came to Carl Mays, though, applying such a metric would have been difficult. The only predictable factor was that he was unpredictable.

The righthanded submariner had something of a tumultuous career, and a personality that by most accounts wasn't always favorable among players and coaches in the big leagues. To make matters even grayer, he was a spitballer. Combined with his unique delivery and blazing fastball, this quirk made him a formidable, if not dangerous pitcher.

Often, Mays would use this reputation to his advantage by intimidating batters to control the strike zone and coercing them into weak contact. But his stigma as a foe to be feared gained significant steam in 1915 during a game that featured a fiery encounter with Ty Cobb and the Detroit Tigers.

Mays, pitching for the Boston Red Sox, reportedly threw at Cobb during each of his at-bats. This enticed Cobb to throw his bat at Mays and ignite a confrontation. Once things calmed down, Mays responded by plunking Cobb on the wrist. [1] Though he may or may not have pitched with intended aggression, he appeared to have no fear or shame. When he was on the mound, he was the boss.

Still with the Red Sox in 1918, Mays and his team were enjoying a fantastic season, one that would end with a World Series Championship over the Chicago Cubs. That year, Mays was the ace on a pitching staff that also included Babe Ruth. He went

---

[1] https://www.smithsonianmag.com/history/a-death-at-home-plate-84826570/

21-13 with a 2.21 ERA, tossing 30 complete games and tacking on eight shutouts over 293 innings pitched.

Early in the season on May 20, an incident occurred which would, in a way, portend an eerie and deadly second act.

In the third inning of an 11-1 rout of the Cleveland Indians at Fenway Park, Mays let loose a pitch that drilled the great Tris Speaker right on the head. Speaker would be okay, but the extreme nature of this beaning only firmed up the frightening reputation that Mays had long carried.

Two years later, a shockingly similar incident – against the same team no less – would end in tragedy.

In keeping pace with the high-high's and low-lows of his career, late in the 1918 season on August 30, Mays became the only pitcher in Red Sox history to throw two complete game wins in the same day. Both wins were integral in keeping the Red Sox atop the pennant hunt as the season went into the final stretch, where they carried onward to win the World Series.

Mays had some rough luck to start 1919, at one point sitting at just 5-11, but with a strong ERA of 2.47 in 21 appearances. He was traded to the New York Yankees where he had a much better second half, going 9-3 with a 1.65 ERA in 13 starts.

In 1920, Mays, still pitching for the Yankees, would play a big part in a truly dark moment in the history of baseball.

On August 16, in the fifth inning of a key game against the Cleveland Indians at the Polo Grounds in New York, tragedy struck. On a 1-1 count, Mays unleashed a fastball that hit Indians shortstop Ray Chapman on the side of his head. The blow dropped him to the ground, knocking him out with a fractured skull. Although Chapman was able to regain consciousness and be helped off the field, he would die early the next morning at the age of 29, the trauma to his head too severe to repair.

Several factors likely contributed to this accident, including the weather and the ball itself.

It was a humid, gloomy, drizzly day in New York, and by the fifth inning the ball would have become dirty and hard to see. In those days, it was common to play most of, if not the entire game, with one ball if it wasn't hit out of play. Even if the pitch was not intended to hit him, or if Chapman was crowding the plate, it's entirely possible that the conditions made it difficult for him to pick up the sight of the ball out of Mays' hand and thus, unable to get out of the way.

In the span of two years, Mays hit two Indians' batters on the head, with one beaning resulting in death. He always vehemently denied throwing at Chapman intentionally. The incident would haunt Mays for the rest of his playing days, and life thereafter.

Some measure of good did come out of it, though.

Chapman's death ignited a series of rules changes that are still in use today. Beginning shortly after the tragedy, umpires began to insert new baseballs into the game when the one in play became scuffed or too dirty. The spitball and other doctored-up pitches were outlawed, and although it took over thirty years to be fully integrated, batting helmets became mandatory at all levels.

Despite the constant mental anguish, Mays' career continued with success on the field.

In 1921, he had the best season of his career when he led the American League in wins (27), winning percentage (.750), games (49), saves (7) and innings pitched (336.2.)

He helped guide the Yankees into the World Series against the New York Giants, but his great season would be marred amid accusations that he was offered a bribe from gamblers to throw Game 4. As the alleged story goes, Mays' wife Marjorie signaled her husband from the stands that she had received the bribe money. Mays, who had been dominant in the game up until then, was now in the bag. He started crossing up his pitch signals and became lackadaisical, allowing the Giants to clobber him and take a lead they would not relinquish [2]

The Giants went on to win that game and eventually the best-of-nine-series, five games to three.

Though cleared of any wrongdoing, the rumors of Mays conspiring with gamblers to fix a World Series game must have felt like gas on the fire to Major League Baseball at the time. The Black Sox scandal of 1919 was still fresh in everyone's minds, and the eight players from that team were officially banned from baseball only months prior to the accusations against Mays.

Mays would pitch until 1929, and, all-told, his numbers were strong in his 15-year career.

---

[2] Lyle Spaz and Steve Steinberg, *1921: The Yankees, The Giants, & the Battle for Baseball Supremacy In New York*

He compiled a lifetime record of 207-126, with 231 complete games, 29 shutouts and a 2.92 ERA. He won 20-plus games five different times, threw over 3,000 innings and earned four World Series rings (1915-16, 1918 Red Sox, 1923 Yankees.)

Still, he has been left out of the Hall of Fame, despite having career statistics that could make him worthy of the achievement. Unfortunately, his unfavorable reputation, combined with his direct involvement in Chapman's death and being under suspicion of throwing a World Series game, are the likely reasons for Mays not being enshrined in Cooperstown.

Eighth Inning

Silence of the Bats: The 1917 White Sox Go Hitless Two Days in a Row

Eighth Inning

Silence of the Bats: The 1917 White Sox Go Hitless Two Days in a Row

The Chicago White Sox enjoyed a figurative and literal banner season in 1917, one of the best in their franchise's long history.

The Pale Hosers from Chicago's south side led the American League in attendance at seven-year-old Comiskey Park, finished with a stellar record of 100-54 to take the American League pennant, and then went on to defeat the powerful New York Giants four games to two in the World Series.

When all was said and done, the "Old Roman," team owner Charles Comiskey, could not have been happier with his boys on the field, the cashflow at his ticket windows, and the new championship hardware on display in his famous Bard's Room at his ballpark. But long before the World Series trophy appeared in his private sanctuary at 35th & Shields, Commy's crew had to navigate through a bit of a rocky start.

In a season rife with promise, the White Sox found themselves with just an 11-10 mark, two and a half games out of first place, on May 6. Though still quite early, the struggles were burdensome and noticeable.

Even worse for the White Sox, this date would carry a touch of infamy as their formidable batsmen had just been inexplicably no-hit for the second straight day by, of all teams, the hapless St. Louis Browns.

White Sox skipper Clarence "Pants" Rowland took his squad southwest on what was originally a four-game series at venerable Sportsman's Park against the Browns. Due to two earlier rainouts, however, the Saturday-Wednesday tilt was extended to *six* games. As such, the teams played doubleheaders on Sunday and Tuesday.

The extended series opened on Saturday, May 5th with a little slap of controversy.

Famed White Sox hurler Eddie Cicotte took the bump against Ernie Koob, a 24-year old lefty from Keeler, Michigan in his third year in the bigs. Koob was a bit erratic with his control and only played in four major league seasons, but he still amassed a solid lifetime ERA of 3.13. The May 6 edition of the *Chicago Tribune* erroneously printed the news stating that the White Sox were one-hit the day before. This misprint resulted from the official scorer at Sportsman's Park initially recording a hit on what seemed like an error in the opening frame.

With one out in the top of the first inning, White Sox third baseman Buck Weaver smacked a grounder toward Browns second baseman Ernie Johnson. The 29-year old, who came up with the White Sox in 1912 and would re-join them from 1921-23, was making his first Browns start for the nicked up Del Pratt, who was considered among the best second-sackers in the American League at the time.

Johnson played a bad hop in the muddy field correctly, keeping the ball in front of him with plenty

94

of time to get Weaver at first. But the mucked-up ball slipped from his hand on his attempted throw to future Hall of Fame first baseman George Sisler, and it flipped behind him – a clear error. How anyone could have thought otherwise is a mystery, but somehow the action of the play was confused, ruled a hit, and newspaper accounts followed. [1]

After the game, the official scorer, John Sheridan, sought input from anyone who saw the play – umpires, coaches, and some players. The majority felt the play was in fact an error, and the official record was changed. This prompted the *Baseball Writers Association of America* to file a protest with the American and National Leagues and set forth a mandate that the official scorer cannot reverse a decision unless a clear violation of the rules was evident. [2]

With no video or instant replay available in those days, the official ruling had to rely on the

---

[1]   https://sabr.org/gamesproj/game/may-5-1917-second-thought-its-no-hitter-ernie-koob
[2] sabr.org

combined interpretations of witnesses who saw the play.

In the end, the reversed ruling stood.

Cicotte battled to the very end, allowing five hits, and striking out three in the effort.

The Browns' Koob out-dueled the would-have-been Hall of Famer though, and his gem became the first Browns no-hitter at Sportsman's Park.

As the morning papers with the inaccurate recap landed on doorsteps in Chicago on Sunday, May 6, the first of two doubleheaders in the White Sox/Browns extended series was getting underway in St. Louis.

In the first game, the St. Louis offense peppered White Sox starter Reb Russel for five runs in 3.2 innings and they never looked back. Though the Sox would do some makeup damage against the Browns' Allan Sothoron, they couldn't fully close the gap, and St. Louis ended up the 8-4 victors. Bob

Groom tossed the six-out finish for Fielder Jones' Brownies, throwing two innings of no-hit ball.

But Groom wasn't done yet – not by a long shot.

The Belleville, Illinois native had a fair 10-year career, all in the American League, spending time with the Washington Senators, St. Louis Browns, and Cleveland Indians. His professional life also included a two-year stint with the St. Louis Terriers of the short-lived Federal League. For his career, Groom won 119 games and compiled a 3.10 ERA. To this he added 157 complete games in 288 starts – nothing to frown at by any stretch.

Groom took the mound in the second game of the doubleheader and picked up right where he left off in the opener, going the distance in a 3-0 no-hitter while striking out four.

Opposing him in the nightcap was the White Sox's Joe Benz, a veteran righty on the far backend of the rotation who only appeared in 19 games during the 1917 season. Benz was stout on this day though, going the full game, but allowing three earned runs on eight scattered hits.

For Groom, his 11 consecutive innings of no-hit ball on the same day was a career highlight and added a shiny finish to the sheer oddity of a team – any team – no-hitting the potent White Sox on back to back days.

The doubleheader sweep gave the Browns a decent start at 11-8. Their winning ways wouldn't last though, as they trudged to a 57-97 record by season's end, good for seventh place in the eight-team American League.

The White Sox on the other hand bounced back immediately.

They took the next three games in the series with the Browns to feel a little brighter-eyed at 14-10 and more bushy-tailed at 1.5 games back. They would race on from there to the century mark in wins, capture the American League flag and then nab a World Series championship to finish the year.

Ninth Inning

The Great Zim, Cocky Collins, and One Daring Dash for the Dish

Ninth Inning

The Great Zim, Cocky Collins, and One Daring Dash for the Dish

October 15, 1917, the Polo Grounds. World Series Game 6: New York Giants vs. Chicago White Sox.

More than a century after the White Sox took the deciding game this series, certain elements of one particular, pivotal play, remain mysterious.

The play in question being the Giants' botched rundown of White Sox star Eddie Collins in the top of the fourth inning. This led to the winning run of the series, and cemented Giants third baseman Heinie Zimmerman as the series' scapegoat.

But is that an unfair label?

Zimmerman was a stalwart, but maligned infielder in the latter days of his career in 1917 and certainly no stranger to implication. Throughout his

100

13 years in the big leagues, Zimmerman was often found in questionable situations of all sorts, and he earned a reputation as a ballplayer who never became quite as good as he should have been. [1]

His subpar play in the World Series of 1917 only served to fuel additional talk about where his efforts truly were. In the six game series, he batted just .120 and committed three errors, the last of which came in the form of a costly throwing error that allowed Eddie Collins to reach first base in the crucial fourth inning of the sixth game. Collins would subsequently score the winning run on the infamous chase to the plate.

Most rundowns seem like a rather routine play, but there's a lot to unpack when you look at how this particular one went down.

The wacky rundown

In the top of the fourth with Collins on first following Zimmerman's throwing gaffe, Shoeless Joe

[1] http://sabr.org/bioproj/person/e73e465a

Jackson stepped to the plate and lifted a fly ball toward Giants right fielder Dave Robertson. The 27-year old from Portsmouth, Virginia misjudged the ball, allowing Collins to race around to third while Jackson advanced to second. The next batter, White Sox slugger Happy Felsch, chopped a grounder right back to pitcher Rube Benton. The big righty wheeled and threw behind Collins to Zimmerman at third base, trying to hang Collins up when he shuffled toward home.

This set up the famous rundown.

The pickle apparently started normally, until Collins slipped right past catcher Bill Rariden, who was caught too far up the third base line. Inexplicably, first baseman Walter Holke did not cover the plate. Zimmerman was thus forced to chase Collins all the way home to try and apply a tag.

Collins, the faster runner, beat Zimmerman to the dish, giving the White Sox a lead that they would hold for the rest of the game. This one strange play proved to be the deciding run in the series.

In the century-plus since the famous mad dash, opinions seem to vary on what Rariden actually did, and why.

Most accounts generally agree that once the rundown began in earnest, he took a throw from Zimmerman and began to inch Collins back toward third – the normal thing to do – and he then threw the ball back to Zimmerman at some point. The longer he waited to throw it back, however, the further he would have been up the line and close to Collins, as the two men neared third base. With Jackson holding at second and Felsch at first, Collins wasn't being forced toward home. So, if the Giants couldn't tag him out, then checking him back to third would be their only resort.

The most likely way in which Collins was able to get past Rariden was if he broke for home in perfect timing as Rariden threw the ball back to Zimmerman in the opposite direction. (Depending how close they were, a fake throw by Rariden here could have caught Collins in a standstill.) This too, would not be unusual – except that home plate was mysteriously left open. Collins must have seen the unattended plate and executed a perfect baserunning maneuver under Rariden's throw to reach it.

Other viewpoints seem to suggest that Rariden was hardly engaged in the rundown at all, having bolted up the third base line immediately, *before* waiting for a throw from Zimmerman. This would have left Zimmerman with nobody to throw to from the outset after he took the initial check throw from Benton. That would have been particularly strange if Rariden ran up the third base line on a grounder back to the pitcher who was checking the runner at third.

Therefore, the most probable scenario is that Benton threw to Zimmerman at third, who threw ahead of Collins to Rariden at home, who then inched Collins back toward third, and threw it back to Zimmerman – right as Collins ducked the throw and sprinted for home with Zimmerman in pursuit.

The real mystery then, perhaps lies in why nobody else was covering the plate behind Rariden.

Given that this was long before video replay, and sportswriters in those days had to rely on others' interpretations if they missed seeing the live play themselves, the exact details of what happened may never be fully revealed.

So, where the hell was everybody?

In that rundown situation, with the catcher and third baseman engaged with the runner in-between them, the question becomes why didn't Walter Holke, or maybe even Benton if he decided to (unconventionally) not follow his own throw to third, cover the plate?

There should have been at least one, and possibly *two,* backups for catcher Bill Rariden at home plate after he exited the line when he threw the ball back to Zimmerman. Once Rariden was out of the play, Zimmerman had nobody ahead of him to throw to. He reportedly quipped after the game

"Who the hell was I supposed to throw to, (umpire Bill) Klem?" [2]

And Zimmerman was right.

Even Giants manager John McGraw believed either Holke or Benton should have been covering the plate, but the fans and sportswriters alike would continue to blame Zimmerman for the broken play, doubling down on his poor series, his crucial error early in the inning that put the winning run on, and a string of insinuations and questionable actions throughout his career.

The eyebrow-raising would continue about Zimmerman the next two years, especially after first baseman and master game-fixer Hal Chase, formerly of the Cincinnati Reds, would join the Giants in 1919.

McGraw, taking a flyer on signing Chase in an effort to keep the talented player on the level, would see the plan backfire as Chase and

---

[2] https://sabr.org/bioproj/person/bill-rariden/

Zimmerman formed a potent betting duo. A grand jury was convened to investigate gambling in baseball in 1920, and McGraw and other Giants players would testify to Zimmerman and Chase's agendas for fixing games in 1919.

In the wake of the famous Black Sox scandal, Judge Kenesaw Mountain Landis, early in his tenure as Commissioner of Baseball, banned Chase from the game, and blacklisted Zimmerman in a similar fashion. [3]

The sad tale of Heinie Zimmerman remains an interesting piece of baseball history.

The snafu'd rundown in the last game of the 1917 World Series, along with his lackluster play in the first five games and the key error on Collins' grounder which led to the deciding run, essentially made Zimmerman the fall guy in New York. He would long be mentioned in the same vein as other infamous Giants like Fred Merkle and Fred Snodgrass, having to vehemently deny any

---

[3] https://sabr.org/bioproj/person/heinie-zimmerman/

accusations that he allowed Collins to score on purpose.

Although his reputation of never fulfilling his great potential drew the ire of fans and reporters alike – and his sidekicking with Hal Chase certainly didn't help his stature in the game – he should at least not be to blame for the pivotal rundown in the 1917 Series. He did have a costly error that put the eventual winning run on base. But in the deciding play, he made the only play he could've made.

Unfortunately, the extenuating circumstances surrounding him, and that series, made him take the blame right on the chin.

Extra Innings: The 10ᵗʰ

Ruth's Mysterious Gambit: The Final Out of the 1926 World Series

Ruth's Mysterious Gambit: The Final Out of the 1926 World Series

The 1927 New York Yankees are locked in baseball lore as being arguably the best team of all time.

Often overlooked, however, is the fact they were pretty darn good the previous year, too.

Behind the slugging of Babe Ruth and Lou Gehrig, the '27 Bronx Bombers wrote their own fantastic chapter in baseball history. But the Yankees of '26 were a powerful team in their own right. They captured the American League pennant after a 91-63 campaign and had their sights set on winning their second championship in three years.

Another fate emerged, however, when the St. Louis Cardinals bested them in the seven game series.

The dramatic final out of the last game which gave the Cardinals the crown has been somewhat of a head scratcher for nearly 100 years.

The stage was set for the classic scene on October 10, 1926 at Yankee Stadium: It was the bottom of the ninth in Game 7 of the World Series, the Yankees were up to bat with two outs, and down by a run – the type of situation that every neighborhood kid playing ball in the back yard dreamed about being the hero of.

The setup for this grand finale, however, began two innings earlier.

Veteran Cardinals pitcher Grover Cleveland "Old Pete" Alexander, one day removed from his dazzling complete game victory in Game 6, came on in relief in the bottom of the seventh with two outs and the bases loaded. The aging righty proceeded to strike out future Yankees Hall of Famer Tony Lazzeri to end the inning and squash the Yankees' rally, stunning the overflow crowd at Ruth's House. A truly huge moment.

With a precious 3-2 lead, Cardinals player-manager Rogers Hornsby stayed with his hot hand and kept Alexander in the game. The old hurler chugged along in damage-less fashion to the bottom of the ninth with the top of the Yankees' powerful order coming up.

The 38,000-plus in the stands at then-new Yankee Stadium were hoping for some of those back yard heroics.

Old Pete kept rolling as he forced both Earle Combs and Mark Koenig into groundouts, bringing up Babe Ruth with two outs and nobody on. Ruth battled the righthander to a full count, and then, to the relief of the Yankee faithful, drew a walk.

This brought left fielder Bob Meusel to the plate with the great Lou Gehrig on deck and Lazzeri in the hole – an ideal combination for a rally to tie or win the game.

Even with two outs, the Yankees were probably still feeling pretty decent about their chances. They knew Meusel would get a pitch to hit.

Alexander wasn't going to pitch around him and put the winning run on base with one of the greatest hitters of all time in Gehrig at the plate.

With two away in the inning, he had to go right after Meusel.

The chance for any Yankee magic gave way to baffling gallantry, however. On an Alexander pitch to Meusel, Ruth shockingly broke for second in an attempted two-out delayed steal.

A laser-perfect throw from catcher Bob O'Farrell, the National League MVP in 1926, to Hornsby covering second, nailed Ruth, ending the game and series. St. Louis held on to claim their first World Championship in an excellently played fall classic. [1]

Ruth's attempted steal, particularly in that situation, raise a few questions.

---

[1] https://sabr.org/gamesproj/game/october-10-1926-pete-alexander-saves-the-day/

Did he get caught shuffling out too far on his secondary lead and just tried to reach second instead of inciting a snap throw back from O'Farrell? Or was he just being too aggressive? He *did* steal on O'Farrell the day before, but why the two-out gamble with the heart of the order up?

Some believe that the hit-and-run was on, though neither Ruth, Meusel, or manager Miller Huggins ever fully confirmed that. Did Ruth not believe that Meusel could knock one in the gap or out of the park? This is a possibility since Meusel was reputed to have dips in confidence – but he had hit a double and a triple off Alexander the previous day.

Alexander was in fine form again this day, though, and Meusel had two costly misplays in the fourth inning, including a dropped routine fly ball which directly contributed to all three Cardinals runs in the game.

These things, combined with his inconsistency at the plate (he only hit .238 for the series), no doubt put great strain on Meusel in that situation. Knowing this, perhaps Ruth wanted to put some of the pressure on himself? If so, it was a selfless, but high-risk ploy with two outs.

Or was it something else?

Speculation of one possible, if farfetched, explanation has ties to other significant situations that dotted the landscape of Major League Baseball at the time.

Although unlikely, one thing should be considered in order to properly frame this situation. Rumors were rampant in those days, so it should be no surprise that it has been suggested that Meusel may have been approached by, or accepted payoffs from, gamblers prior to the series. If Meusel was in on some kind of arrangement, it would lend some credence to his uncharacteristic, and timely, defensive mishaps in the game.

In addition, famous betting ringleader Joseph "Sport" Sullivan, a key figure in the fixing of the 1919 World Series was seen in attendance at Yankee

Stadium that day. His presence roused further suspicions of crooked involvement, and he was removed from the stadium by American League President Ban Johnson. [2]

Of course, any speculation of collusion with gamblers at the time was likely – and conveniently – hindsight, but it is interesting to ponder. Gambling and fixing games were everyday subjects among baseball talk in those days.

Just five years removed from eight members of the Chicago White Sox being banned from the game for fixing the 1919 World Series, a flurry of circumstantial evidence surfaced from an accusation by retired Detroit Tigers pitcher Dutch Leonard that superstars Ty Cobb, Tris Speaker and Smoky Joe Wood had fixed a game(s) back in September 1919 between the Tigers and the Cleveland Indians. [3]

Although those accusations were eventually considered to stem from a personal vendetta

---

[2] https://sabr.org/bioproj/person/sport-sullivan/

[3] Timothy Gay, *Tris Speaker: The Rough and Tumble Life of a Baseball Legend*

Leonard had toward Cobb and Speaker, it could open one's eye to bigger picture possibilities. If star players like Cobb and Speaker were not immune to direct exposure to gambling elements, then it's not unrealistic to imagine that a player like Meusel – or even Ruth – could have been approached about not playing this deciding game on the level.

The evidence against Cobb and Speaker gained enough momentum that, just weeks after the 1926 season ended, they both announced their retirement as player-managers at the urging of Johnson, lest the story fully break and possibly destroy two Hall of Fame careers.

The Cobb/Speaker ultimatum was the design of both Johnson and Commissioner Kenesaw Mountain Landis. Even though both men were cleared of any wrongdoing, the potential for collateral damage was obvious. With baseball itself on trial, in a manner of speaking, for most of the 1920's, it would've been crushing, perhaps even fatal for the sport if it were revealed that two megastar players were found to be fixing and betting on games.

Landis realized this danger to the game itself and relented, ceasing his own investigation. Historian Glenn Stout compared Landis' actions in this case to a "seamstress pulling a single thread, only to discover she's unraveling the fabric of the whole garment." [4]

Dismissing the case was an effort to protect the game by hiding this blemish, even if it was at the sake of Landis' own integrity.

Both Cobb and Speaker would ultimately return to baseball the following year with the Philadelphia Athletics and Washington Senators, respectively, in player-coach roles.

For the 1928 season, the aging ballplayers would be united on the Athletics before retiring permanently. Their presence for that one season helped shape a powerhouse team, as Connie Mack's A's would go on to win the World Series in 1929 and 1930.

---

[4] Gay

The situation with Cobb and Speaker, although having no direct involvement with the 1926 Series, is nonetheless important to consider because it was part of the baseball landscape of the time. If two of the game's most heralded stars could be involved with betting on games, not to mention what happened with the Black Sox scandal, then so could anyone – including Bob Meusel or the great Babe Ruth.

There really are no concrete conclusions.

Like so many great or tragic situations in baseball history, the further we delve into them the more questions tend to arise.

Was Ruth just trying to put the game on his shoulders? Did Huggins employ a gutsy hit-and-run that failed? Did Meusel put on the hit-and-run himself and then didn't protect Ruth? Was it just an unbeatable throw by O'Farrell? Were there outside factors like fixing that got to Meusel which affected the outcome of the game?

Whatever the truth may be, this series, and the 1920's as a whole, was a fascinating and dangerous time for Major League Baseball.

Extra Innings: The 11th

Johnson vs. Williams: The Forgotten Duel of 1918

Extra Innings: The 11ᵗʰ

<u>Johnson vs. Williams: The Forgotten Duel of 1918</u>

The year of 1918 was a tumultuous and frightening time in the world.

With the population's attention and emotions enveloped by both the first World War and the Spanish Flu pandemic, baseball in America continued on, but with less vigor than usual.

Largely forgotten early in that season was a game on May 15 where the Washington Senators beat the defending World Champion Chicago White Sox 1-0 in an 18-inning thriller at Griffith Stadium. In true Deadball Era fashion, the twice-as-long contest still only took just 2 hours and 43 minutes to complete.[1]

---

[1] https://ghostsofdc.org/2014/05/12/time-walter-johnson-pitched-18-innings-one-game/

A low-scoring pitchers' duel was certainly nothing new in those latter days of the Deadball Era, but what happened in this particular game is worth a closer look, if only to acknowledge the greatness that transpired.

Young White Sox starter Claude "Lefty" Williams, a superb control pitcher who would be banned from the game three years later for his involvement in the infamous 1919 World Series, squared off against future Hall of Famer Walter "Big Train" Johnson.

The two pitchers duplicated each other's wizardry for the entire game, as both went the distance in the 18-inning affair.

The winning run finally crossed the plate in the bottom of the 18th. Johnson himself had a big hand in getting the deciding tally across.

Senators' catcher Eddie "Dorf" Ainsmith started the game-clinching rally off.

The stalwart journeyman backstop, who played 15 years in the big leagues with the Senators,

Detroit Tigers, St. Louis Cardinals, Brooklyn Dodgers and New York Giants, hit a one-out single to center.

This brought up Johnson, who then also singled to center field. Aggressive baserunning by Ainsmith landed him on third when he perceived a momentary indecisive step by White Sox center fielder Shano Collins, after he corralled Johnson's hit.[2]

The Senators sensed that victory was at hand, though maybe not in the particular fashion it would occur.

With runners on first and third and still only one out, leadoff man and right fielder Burt Shotton stepped into the box. He worked Williams to a 1-1 count, before Williams uncorked what the Washington Herald called a "wild heave"[3] behind catcher Ray Schalk. The costly mistake sent

[2] https://chroniclingamerica.loc.gov/lccn/
[3] Chroniclingamerica.loc.gov

Ainsworth across the plate and the Senators to the win.

Although suffering the loss, Williams was extremely efficient. He went 17.1 innings in the affair, scattering just eight hits and striking out five. To lose the game on a wild pitch after turning in such a lengthy, valiant outing must have been angering.

Johnson, for his part, turned in one of his classic stellar performances.

He scattered 10 hits in the 18-frame affair, while striking out nine of the robust White Sox hitters, who were without sluggers Shoeless Joe Jackson and Happy Felsch due to their wartime duties.

For an early game in an overlooked season, this one was a true gem for both teams. Two dominant pitchers make the game's totals tell of a tight, evenly matched contest: 18 innings. 18 hits. One run. Less than three hours to complete.

The Senators glided to a strong 72-56 record and third-place finish in the tightly contested American League pennant race. They completed their campaign two and a half games behind the runner-up Cleveland Indians, and four games behind the American League and eventual World Series Champion Boston Red Sox.

The White Sox, although the defending champs in 1918, struggled with many key players missing significant games due to wartime responsibilities. They limped to a 57-67 mark, 17 games back in 6th place in the American League.

The following season would live on in baseball infamy when the Cincinnati Reds beat the White Sox five games to three in the World Series, a fall classic forever remembered as the Black Sox scandal.

Williams was one of the players involved in throwing the series, and he, along with seven of his teammates, were ultimately banned from the game in 1921.

One unconnected, though fascinating twist of ironic foreshadowing, however, occurred four years before that fateful series.

Hugh Fullerton, one of the nation's leading syndicated baseball writers at the time and mostly remembered as being one of the chief exposers of the scandal, inadvertently and fictitiously prophesied Williams' fate.

In 1915, he wrote a novel about baseball and one of the characters, a left-handed pitcher named Williams, is bribed by a group of gamblers to purposely tank the pennant. [4]

A total coincidence? Yes. But a fascinating parallel, nonetheless.

---

[4] https://sabr.org/bioproj/person/lefty-williams/

The 1919 World Series: Did the White Sox Lose, Or Did the Reds Win?

Extra Innings: The 12th

The 1919 World Series: Did the White Sox Lose, Or Did the Reds Win?

It has been over 100 years since eight (arguably six) members of the Chicago White Sox conspired with gamblers to throw the 1919 World Series to the Cincinnati Reds.

The White Sox of 1919 were considered by some to be one of the best teams of all time, at least of the Deadball Era, and heavy favorites to win the nine-game series over the Reds.

The rest is history.

Exceedingly gray history, that is.

If you ask many people, even those only casually familiar with the story, they'd probably say that the White Sox would've easily won that World Series and they just tanked it on purpose.

But is it really as simple as that?

129

The eight accused members of the White Sox were officially banned from baseball in 1921, and ever since, ceaseless research continues on to try and determine what really happened that fateful October more than a century ago.

Eight Men Out, the famous 1963 book by Eliot Asinof (and the 1988 film of the same name by John Sayles), had long been regarded as one of the more accepted takes on the story. Over time, however, more detailed, and accurate facts have surfaced which discredit a lot of Asinof's book. Both book and film, while entertaining and compelling, paint a much too broad and often unsubstantiated stroke of the truth. By comparison, Gene Carney's 2006 book, *Burying the Black Sox*, is a far more authoritative and factual piece than Asinof's effort could ever claim to be.

But the main problem when looking at this story is that it becomes something of an unending cycle of mysteries – the more facts that come to the surface, the more questions arise.

Some believe that the entire 1919 World Series was fixed from the start. Others ascertain that somewhere around the third or fourth game when the accused White Sox players did not receive their promised bribe money, they began to try to win. Yet others still would say that one of the chief tragedies (among many) in that series, is that the Cincinnati Reds have never fully received their due credit as a team capable of beating the White Sox in a nine-game marathon.

The truth, as with many debatable things, is probably somewhere in the middle.

In taking a closer look, we see there is much evidence showing that the 1919 Reds were certainly no fluke, and although anything can happen in baseball, they very well could have been *better* than the mighty White Sox.

Cincinnati took the National League pennant with an impressive record of 96-44. They were a balanced team with an excellent infield and consistent, if not spectacular, starting pitching. The betting odds were heavily in Chicago's favor prior to the start of the series but leveled off before the first game when leaked rumors of the fix reached bettors' ears. It's important to remember that in that era, fixing games and betting on baseball were as common as they were shady. Major League Baseball already had several players on the official banned list by 1919 for such acts, so there was plenty of precedent to keep a keen eye on this series.

The flurry of rumors and hearsay about a fix turned this matchup between two polarizing clubs on its head before a single pitch was even thrown.

Organizationally and internally, the Reds and White Sox were night and day different from one another. Statistically and measurably, however, they drew some rather interesting comparisons in several important categories that may dull some of the polish off the White Sox.

As a team, the White Sox were overall better hitters than the Reds and their star power gave them a slight edge, intangibly, in terms of prestige. Despite the irony that it was that very star power which caused disharmony and contributed to the personal division of the team, they still carried three Hall of Fame players on the roster in catcher Ray Schalk, second baseman Eddie Collins and pitcher Red Faber.

Conceivably, that number could've been as high as *eight* if the ban didn't happen.

Shoeless Joe Jackson was a lock for Cooperstown. An argument could've been made for Eddie Cicotte as it were. Lefty Williams, Buck Weaver, and Happy Felsch were all just getting into their prime years with bright futures ahead of them. If their career trajectories stayed on course, they were likely to put up significant numbers along with the potential for multiple championship rings.

With two pennants in three years and leading the pennant race late into the 1920 season before the suspension of eight key players, the White Sox as a team were on the verge of a dynasty as well.

The Reds meanwhile had just one future Hall of Famer on their club in outfielder Edd Rousch, but what they may have lacked in accolades and stature, they more than made up for by being a disciplined, well-rounded team.

The Reds' lack of glamour made them seem underrated compared to the more prominent White Sox. Added to which, recency bias from sportswriters and fans enhanced these perceptions further. Heading into the 1919 series, American League teams had won eight of the previous nine championships, including the White Sox two years' prior in 1917. These facts fueled the American League's reputation of dominance, but it could have also given the impression that the White Sox were better than they really were.

As with any postseason series, even today, one of the biggest keys was the starting pitching. The Reds carried a huge advantage there. What it boiled down to was simply that the Reds had a full, healthy rotation, and the White Sox did not.

Starting pitching depth is crucial to a long series, and Cincinnati was able to attack Chicago with a strong five-man barrage consisting of Dutch Ruether, Slim Sallee, Ray Fisher, Jimmy Ring and Hod Eller. The White Sox only had three healthy arms ready to go, and more like two if Cicotte's reported arm soreness was a factor.[1]

The tangible correlations between the two clubs become rather compelling from there.

On the season, the Reds pitching staff cached a team ERA of 2.23, compared to the White Sox's 3.04. The trend in this disparity is even more significant when you consider the Reds had a full rotation, whereas the White Sox were stretched far too thin. They had to rely on Cicotte and Williams to carry the load, with each man having to make three starts in the series.

---

[1] https://sabr.org/bioproj/person/eddie-cicotte/

One other major factor working against the White Sox that isn't mentioned often in the narrative of the scandal is about pitcher Red Faber.

The Hall of Fame right hander posted an 11-9 mark with a 3.83 ERA for the season, but that was mostly in the first half. He battled constant illness and injuries down the stretch and was unavailable for the entire series. Had he been able to go, the complexion of the White Sox rotation would have shifted considerably.

In place of Faber, rookie Dickey Kerr, theretofore unproven in big games despite having an excellent regular season (13-7, 2.88 ERA), had to step up big time. The little lefty did just that, winning the two games he started and keeping the White Sox alive throughout the series, but it wasn't enough.

That Cicotte and Williams were in on the fix didn't change the fact that Cincinnati had more, better, and rested arms. Thus, the pitching advantage, without question, went to the Reds.

Defensively, the Reds had an edge over the White Sox, too.

On the season, Cincinnati had less errors and a higher fielding percentage than their Chi-town counterparts. Additionally, the Reds compiled 23 shutouts on the season to the White Sox's 14. This can logically be attributed to a combination of great pitching and defense. While the White Sox certainly had their share of both, they often relied on their 'big inning' offense [2] to score runs in bunches and bail them out of many games.

Conversely, the Reds made evident the time-honored belief that good pitching beats good hitting...most of the time. Defensive advantage to the Reds here.

A better defense and healthier rotation weren't the only assets the Reds carried into the series.

---

[2] *The 1919 Reds: Requiem for the Robbed* by Jeff Kallman in SABR's *Black Sox Scandal Research Committee Newsletter vol 10 No. 2, December 2018*

Heading down the stretch run of the regular season, the Reds were also the hotter and hungrier team. They went 47-19 in the second half of the season compared to the Sox's 40-26 mark, and only lost twice in September vs. the other teams involved in the National League pennant race (New York Giants, Chicago Cubs, Pittsburgh Pirates). The White Sox, meanwhile, were just .500 in that same month vs. the New York Yankees, Cleveland Indians, and Detroit Tigers, all of whom were fighting for the American League banner. [3]

Against the contending teams in the National League throughout the season, Cincinnati wound up with a strong mark of 38-22, whereas the White Sox went 35-25 against the top squads in the American League. The Reds took the National League pennant in cruise-control fashion with a nine-game cushion over the Giants. The White Sox's sprint to the finish line was closer though, as they captured the

---

[3] Kallman

American League flag by three and a half games over the Indians.[4]

Essentially, what this means is that the Reds played better against the best teams in the National League than the White Sox did against the best in the American League.

The Reds had more success in key games. They showcased better pitching and defense throughout the year and had a full staff of capable arms at their disposal in October. The White Sox could claim *none* of that heading into the World Series of 1919.

As we know however, the stats don't always tell the full story.

One of, or perhaps *the* biggest advantage the Reds had over the White Sox cannot be measured or represented by any metric: They didn't despise one another.

---

[4] Kallman

This is where intangibles like team chemistry come in to play, and the White Sox had a much harder ship to steer than the Reds did in that regard. With their clubhouse essentially divided into two cliques, the White Sox had long dealt with dissention. This was well before the gamblers' influence in fixing the series became the gas thrown on the proverbial fire.

What makes deciphering the scandal such a mess (a century later or not), was that it was a mess in itself at the time.

Nobody will ever know the *real* truth because even the players themselves didn't fully know – or didn't want to know – what was going on. The Reds heard the rumors but shooed them off, and instead focused on winning games. For the White Sox, it was always unclear, even among the team, who was really trying to win and who wasn't, and who may have been double-crossing who.

Imagine being in that clubhouse with all the uncertainty!

Those doubts alone would presumably cast major mental anguish on a ballplayer. How could they look their teammates in the eye? What could they say without sounding paranoid at best or like an untrusting rat at worst? Not to mention the constant barrage of questions from teammates, manager Kid Gleason, owner Charles Comiskey, reporters, and fans, which must have added to the distractions and intrateam discontent.

All of this likely impaired the White Sox's ability to be *mentally* ready to play in the series. Sure, they managed to deal with their personal differences throughout the season and reach the World Series, but the discord was reaching critical mass by this point.

Individually, the "Clean Sox" players, plus guys like Jackson and Weaver – who were in on *discussions* of the fix, but their excellent play and stout denials of actual involvement indicated they were trying to win – must have gone through hell trying to play while unsure of their teammates' real intentions.

Jackson, for his part, while playing flawless ball, still accepted $5,000 in bribe money for his role. Despite his attempts to return the money and deny his involvement, he always carries that red thumb, even long after his death.

While this all gives plenty of credence to a case of the White Sox beating themselves, that does not – and should not – discredit Cincinnati's efforts.

In a way, it was a near-perfect storm for the Reds.

In one clubhouse, there was a team full of stars, but who were divided, leaderless, unhealthy, and mistrusting of one another. This was all *before* several key players conspired to fix games.

In the other, there was a team who had chemistry, balance, physical and mental health, and a hunger to win.

Which team sounds more ready to compete in an extended series?

The Reds just had to go and play their own game, and, as heavy underdogs, really had nothing to lose. These things alone could conceivably lighten the challenge they faced.

Speculation will always remain. Did the Reds catch the White Sox at the worst possible time as they were tearing themselves apart from within? Or were they actually the better team?

No matter what, the Reds of 1919 were no slouch, and that should not be overlooked.

Extra Innings: The 13th

Mathewson's Monumental Marvel of 1905

Extra Innings: The 13th

Mathewson's Monumental Marvel of 1905

The New York Giants sure had a swell season in 1905.

Actually, it was tremendous, and the way it ended was ridiculous.

If a modern-day pitcher throws crucial postseason innings on short rest, they often get a certain praise bestowed upon them. If they make rare appearances on consecutive days, they will gain even more renown.

What happened with the Giants at the end of the 1905 season though, especially if you compare it to today's pitching standards, is truly amazing.

The famous, feisty skipper John McGraw led his New York club to a staggering 105-48 record in the 1905 season. This campaign included a June 29 game in Brooklyn that featured a now-famous half-inning appearance by a rookie outfielder named Archibald "Moonlight" Graham.

The Giants went on to capture the National League pennant by nine games over the Pittsburgh Pirates, and then drubbed Connie Mack's powerful Philadelphia Athletics four games to one in the second-ever World Series.

What makes this series so interesting, well over a century later, is that it featured the most incredible multi-game performance by a starting pitcher – ever – in a World Series.

His name was Christy Mathewson.

Pitching was the name of the game in the Deadball Era, and 1905 saw a slew of it, especially that which was doled out by the New York Giants.

Led by Mathewson, this gritty team from Manhattan had a starting rotation so strong that the number *five* man, lefthander Hooks Wiltse, compiled a 15-6 record with a 2.47 ERA in 197 innings. He fired 18 complete games and carried a WHIP of just over 1. A pitcher in today's game with

146

such numbers would be a finalist for the Cy Young Award, if not the outright winner.

Of the five-man rotation, Hall of Famer Joe McGinnity had the highest ERA at just 2.87. To this he added 21 wins and 26 complete games in 38 starts, while throwing 320.1 innings (which pales in comparison to the 408 he threw in 1904 or the 434 in 1903.) The rest of the rotation – Red Ames (22-8, 2.74) and Dummy Taylor (16-9, 2.66), both put up similar outlandish numbers.

The Giants only carried six pitchers on the roster and had a team ERA of just 2.39. Only 36 of their 153 games were not complete game performances. The lone reliever on the staff, Claude Elliott, appeared in just 10 games, throwing 38 total innings.

It should be noted that as terrific as all their season totals were, they fell far short of Mathewson's individual achievements.

As the ace of the staff, the gentlemanly righthander from Factoryville, PA went 31-9 with a

1.28 ERA and tossed a mammoth 338 innings while completing 32 of 37 games started. He led the league in wins, ERA, shutouts (8), strikeouts (206) and WHIP (0.93).

Still, that's not even the ridiculous part. Mathewson saved that for the World Series.

Throughout the 1905 campaign, Mathewson was regularly unhittable and drew some justified hyperbole by the sportswriters of the day. Damon Runyon, for example, did so quite eloquently:

"Mathewson pitched against Cincinnati yesterday. Another way of putting it is that Cincinnati lost a game of baseball. The first statement means the same as the second."[1]

Although the whole staff was riding the coattails of Mathewson's magic heading into the series, few people could have expected the work that he would turn in. He was virtually untouchable in

---

[1] http://baseballhall.org/discover/inside-pitch/christy-mathewson-throws-third-shutout

Games 1 and 3 of the Fall Classic, blanking the Athletics 3-0 and 9-0 with just three days separating the two shutouts, and he wasn't done there.

With the A's on the verge of defeat, McGraw smelled blood in the water and sent Mathewson to the mound again for Game 5 on less than two full days' rest.

He slung another shutout, out-dueling the Athletics' Chief Bender who had earned the win for Philadelphia in Game 2. The goose-egg of Mack's men at the Polo Grounds secured the title for the Giants and sent New York into a championship frenzy.

McGinnity took the loss in the second game but bounced back to win Game 4, throwing a complete-game shutout of his own. Ames threw one inning of relief in Game 2. Mathewson did everything else.

For the series, his pitching totals were astonishing: 3 starts, 3 wins, 27 innings, 0 runs, 13 hits, 1 walk and 18 strikeouts. He did all this in just five days.

The final scores of each game in this series are interesting, and worth noting. In each of the five contests, the loser was shut out. New York won their games by scores of 3-0, 9-0, 1-0 and 2-0. The lone win for the Athletics was by a tally of 3-0.

In any era of baseball, no one has ever done anything like Mathewson did in the 1905 World Series. It was a hell of an exclamation point on an already stellar season and it's the type of feat, especially considering that it only took a few days to accomplish, that we'll never see again.

Extra Innings: The 14th

A Great Game Seven Finally
Ends the Greatest Drought

Extra Innings: The 14[h]

A Great Game Seven Finally Ends the Greatest Drought

Everyone knew the biggest baseball story in 2016: The Chicago Cubs hadn't won a World Series since 1908 and hadn't appeared in one since 1945.

Many Cubs fans who grew up in the years after World War II often wondered if it would *ever* happen in their lifetime.

Even with a handful of strong teams that had fighting chances in the years since '45, something still never seemed quite right – there was always just *something* missing. Or that even the good teams were never quite opportune enough; an error here; lack of depth there; being on the wrong end of a funny bounce; offense went ice cold...the list went on.

Whatever the magical "it" factor is that every World Series champion seems to have, it eluded the Cubs for more than a century.

Little did anyone know, however, that by 2016 a unique connection was running all the way back through that century-plus that unified the franchise and fans in a special way. But even when the stars *finally* aligned for the north siders in the autumn of that year, it still wasn't without plenty of drama, poetic justice, and more than a plop of irony.

One thing is for sure: generations of Cubs fans had dreamed for far too long to hear the words that many believed might never be announced: "The Cubs win the World Series!"

When that very call finally boomed on TV, radio, and online broadcasts throughout the world, 'surreal' wasn't an accurate enough description of the moment.

Some called it the last great American sports story, and looking back, it just *had* to happen the way it did, didn't it?

Of course, it did.

November 2, 2016.

The 38,104 fans at Cleveland's Progressive Field [1] and the millions more watching and listening around the globe were about to experience some sensational history, one way or another.

It was the fifth inning of Game 7 in what was already widely considered one of the best World Series of all time. The Cubs were holding a fairly comfortable 5-1 lead.

Things were looking quite bright for the Cubs and the pervading thought was that it. Just. Might. Finally. Happen.

Except before any semblance of relaxation could set in, terror struck.

Oh, boy.

With two outs in the fifth inning, Cubs manager Joe Maddon pulled starting pitcher Kyle

---

[1] https://www.baseball-reference.com/boxes/CLE/CLE201611020.shtml

Hendricks. It was a move that drew every reaction from confusion to borderline hatred from fans and is still debated about to this day. Hendricks had thrown just 63 pitches and was cruising along in the rhythm-and-velvet fashion Cubs fans have come to adore of him.

Yanking Hendricks was just the first thing to run askew for the Cubs that night.

Almost immediately, the tides began to turn for the Indians. A rare throwing error from Cubs catcher David Ross, who entered the game when starting pitcher Jon Lester came in from the bullpen, put runners on second and third. A subsequent wild pitch from Lester plated those two runs.

Just like that, the Cubs' cozy lead was no more. Lester got out of the inning, but significant damage had been done.

Hanging on to a now precarious 5-3 lead in the top of the sixth, the grizzly veteran Ross, in his final Major League game as a player, grabbed a key run back when he poetically lit up the scoreboard with a solo home run off Andrew Miller. This made the game 6-3 and brought back an inch of breathing room.

With the blast, Ross became the oldest catcher (39) to homer in a World Series game.

Lester went back out and settled in, tossing three solid innings in relief before giving way to fireballer Aroldis Chapman with two outs in the bottom of the eighth.

Chapman entered Game 7 fighting fatigue from overuse in the previous two games. With everything on the line, Maddon tasked him with getting a three-plus out save on the biggest baseball stage in the world.

He took the mound holding a three-run lead and immediately, terror struck again.

Indians third baseman Jose Ramirez stepped to the plate and lashed a single, to which outfielder Brandon Guyer answered with an RBI double, scoring Ramirez to tighten the score at 6-4.

As the Cleveland faithful were hearing the first subtle notes of heroic euphony, center fielder Rajai Davis strolled to the batter's box. After working up a harrowing 2-2 count, Davis slammed a heater from Chapman into the left field bleachers. The game was now tied at 6 and Progressive Field burst into bedlam.

For the Cubs and their fans, familiar agony had arrived.

The once-steady four-run lead felt like last week's news, hastened by some questionable moves from generally steady Maddon. The collective angst from Cubs fans everywhere (including the author) was palpable.

The rhetorical questions rang both aloud and in silent shock from Cubs fans: *"Is this really happening? And* now *of all times?"*

Chapman finished out the eighth with no additional harm, setting up the tension-riddled ninth inning. Neither team was able to plate a run, so it was quite fitting for a game like this to go to extra innings.

As if to add more drama to the mix, a little divine intervention – perhaps – descended upon Progressive Field in the form of a rain delay. It was a short one at that, only lasting 17 minutes, but it was just enough time to allow the creation of another folkloric moment in the Cubs' universe.

During the deluge, the Cubs players gathered themselves into a small weight room near their clubhouse where Jason Heyward delivered an impassioned speech to his teammates. The perennial Gold Glove right fielder had been under some scrutiny during the season for not putting up offensive numbers befitting of his astronomical contract. But for whatever existing doubts there were of his contractual worth, he more than made up for in his clubhouse and leadership value right then and there. Whatever he said turned out to be exactly what his club needed to hear at precisely the right moment.

When play resumed, the rejuvenated Cubs wasted no time taking charge of the game once more.

A leadoff single in the top of the 10th by designated hitter Kyle Schwarber, returning late in the postseason after suffering a devastating knee injury in early April got things going. Albert Almora, Jr. entered the game to pinch-run for Schwarber, and he promptly turned in arguably the greatest tag-up in Cubs history.

Third baseman Kris Bryant, the National League MVP in 2016, lifted a deep flyball to the warning track in right center. Almora, Jr., tagging from first, picked up on Davis' heeled positioning as he made the catch and broke hard for second, reaching the bag safely. The heads-up hustle play would be akin to Dave Roberts' famous stolen base for the Boston Red Sox in the 2004 American League Championship Series in terms of importance. Cleveland intentionally walked first baseman Anthony Rizzo next, setting up eventual World Series MVP Ben Zobrist with one out and Almora, Jr. in scoring position on second.

The veteran second baseman, who had just won a World Series as a member of the Kansas City

Royals the year before, lanced a double down the third base line to bring home Almora, Jr. and reclaim the lead for the Cubs, 7-6.

With Rizzo now on third and first base sitting open, an intentional walk to shortstop Addison Russell loaded the bases and brought up pinch hitter Miguel Montero with still only one out. The feisty catcher, who's pivotal eighth-inning grand slam made him the hero of Game 1 of the NLCS against the Los Angeles Dodgers, promptly singled home Rizzo to extend the Cubs lead to 8-6.

The offensive burst gave the Cubs control of the game once more, even quicker than they'd just lost it. This was something that fans got used to seeing them do with regularity, while justifying one of the team's many slogan's that season, "We Never Quit."

Cleveland was able to exit the inning with no more runs allowed but would enter the bottom of the 10th on the short end of an 8-6 score.

But of course, this one was far from over.

Cubs relief pitcher Carl Edwards, Jr. replaced Chapman, and set to work on the Indians' batters.

He struck out Mike Napoli, and coerced slugger Jose Ramirez into a groundout. With two away in quick fashion, the Cubs had a World Series championship inches from their grasp.

As if any more suspense could be ladled into the kettle, Edwards, Jr. walked Brandon Guyer to bring up the new Cubs Killer-in-waiting, Rajai Davis. Guyer advanced to second, and Davis lined a single to center, scoring Guyer and cutting the Cubs' lead to 8-7.

The tension at both ballparks (as thousands of Cubs fans had gathered at and around Wrigley Field), in bars, restaurants, and living rooms everywhere was reaching its crescendo.

With two outs and a man on first, the Cubs' versatile swingman pitcher Mike Montgomery entered the game, charged with getting the final out.

Michael Martinez, representing the winning run, stepped to the plate.

On an 0-1 curveball, Martinez nicked a chopper toward Kris Bryant, who was charging in from third. The lanky kid from Las Vegas fielded the ball cleanly but another momentary heart stoppage ensued for all Cubs fans when he slipped slightly in the damp grass while gunning the ball – almost too high for comfort of course – to Anthony Rizzo at first.

Fortunately, the ball hit its target.

The Cubs secured the final out, taking 108 years' worth of championship drought with it.

Cubs fans' own celebratory screams drowned out the famous line they had dreamed of broadcasters calling for so long. That was okay; they'd replay that final out countless times over the coming weeks, months, and years.

The whole spectacle was fitting in ways only the Cubs could conjure up.

They just *had* to scare the crap out of the fans one last time, actually several last times, before making history. In some strange way, it made sense

162

for it to happen like that though. With a four-run lead inching toward the late innings, the game could've gone somewhat vanilla – as vanilla as Game 7 of the World Series between the two teams who'd been without championships the longest could be. But instead, some strange strategic decisions led to a big rally by the home team; a dramatic game-tying homer; a trip to extra innings; a rain delay; an offensive explosion; a lead change; another two-out rally; and then lastly the historic final out.

Sure, why not?

The end result was what many now consider among the greatest baseball games ever played, at least in a World Series.

A victory parade and rally, attended by an estimated 5 million people [2], was held in Chicago a couple days later. It was a glorious celebration over a century in the making.

2

https://www.dnainfo.com/chicago/20161104/downtown/cubs-rally-parade-attendance-5-million/

For Cubs fans, it was not only a euphoric feeling of a championship long overdue, but it was also more than a little vindication.

While baseball folklore and its mythic history are part of the very fabric of the game, some of it is better off gone. With this World Series win, the Cubs and their fans would no longer have to endure any more cliched ridicule; no more friendly (and unfriendly) jabs from other team's fans; no more silly goats; no more mysterious black cat; no more curses; no more "loveable losers" label, and no more "wait until next year."

All of that jargon had gone silent, and for Cubs fans, no silence was ever so pleasantly deafening.

Extra Innings: The 15th

Field of Dreams: Is the
Beloved Classic Really a
Baseball Movie?

- *The following chapter assumes that you've either seen the movie* Field of Dreams, *read the book upon which it's based,* Shoeless Joe, *or both. If neither, then consider these next pages to be chock full of major spoilers.*

Extra Innings: The 15th

Field of Dreams: Is the Beloved Classic Really a Baseball Movie?

As noted earlier, baseball is a game that embraces the absurd.

This is especially true with regard to the storytelling aspect of the game, wherein hyperbole and exaggeration appear with regularity.

It is also why the game of baseball lends itself so seamlessly, no pun intended, to the worlds of fiction and fantastical naturalism.

Authors like Bernard Malamud (*The Natural*), Douglass Wallop (*The Year the Yankees Lost the Pennant*), and W.P. Kinsella (*Shoeless Joe*), were masters of this art, the latter of whom wrote the novel that was adapted into the film which is the focus of this chapter.

This year, 2021, marks the 100th year since eight members of the Chicago White Sox were officially banned from the game for their actions in fixing the infamous 1919 World Series. The tragic tale hasn't slowed down a single beat since then. If anything, more research, writing, and debates are going on about the Black Sox scandal now more than ever.

Over the years, the story made its way to mainstream entertainment with the release of revered movies like *Eight Men Out* and *Field of Dreams.*

Even modern baseball cannot ignore the nostalgic, compelling pull of such stories.

In a case of life imitating art imitating life, MLB scheduled a game for August 12, 2021 between the New York Yankees and Chicago White Sox at the "Field of Dreams", a custom-built ballpark adjacent to the location that was used in the movie of the same name.

While both of these films are considered classics in their own right, there are always some inherent risks that come with book adaptations.

Mostly, these are with regard to accuracy, consistency, and the omnipresent danger of being too "Hollywooded up."

Eight Men Out is a book by Eliot Asinof, first published in 1963. This book, while *basically* true, is actually rife with errors and mostly unsubstantiated claims. Although well-written and compelling, Asinof's book is essentially *his* take on things. He based his story on a lot of conjecture and hearsay rather than reported and accepted facts.[1] The narrative is a decent overview of the scandal and its components, but other books on the subject, such as Gene Carney's *Burying the Black Sox*, provide far more factual details based on meticulous and accurate research.

The 1988 film version of *Eight Men Out* by John Sayles followed suit with Asinof's inconsistencies. In spite of an excellent cast, compelling drama, and realistic action, a significant

---

[1] https://sabr.org/eight-myths-out/appendix

amount of both the book and film versions of *Eight Men Out* are as fictitious as *Field of Dreams*.

Seemingly millions of people hold *Field of Dreams* sacred and have since its release in 1989. As with *Eight Men Out*, this movie is also based on a book, the 1982 novel *Shoeless Joe* by W.P. Kinsella.

Kinsella's forte as a writer was to blend historical fiction with magical realism. This is the foundation of the story, and both his novel and the ensuing film illustrate that ambiance almost perfectly.

The movie features memorable performances from the cast and contains a score by the late James Horner so impactful that the music is virtually a character itself. The film follows the novel quite closely, with baseball being one of the key elements of the story.

There are a few short baseball scenes, some baseball players, and baseball-related dialogue in much of the movie. The first mention of baseball occurs mere seconds into the prologue. Toward the end, James Earl Jones' character Terence Mann delivers a powerful baseball-centric speech that will forever be quoted by current and future generations and used in promo spots on TV and radio. The movie is also regularly shown on cable TV channels, including the *MLB Network.*

Considering all that, is it still really fair, or even accurate, to call *Field of Dreams* a "baseball movie?"

Even with its hovering presence, baseball in *Field of Dreams* is simply not depicted the way it is in other (obvious) baseball movies like *Major League, Bull Durham, The Natural, 61*, 42,* or even *Eight Men Out.*

Why?

That is because baseball is not the plot of *Field of Dreams* – it's only a *plot device.*

It's a means to an end, a component that moves the story along, but it is not the story itself.

Not even close, in fact.

Baseball is one of the many big themes present in the film, but that doesn't necessarily mean it technically qualifies as a "baseball movie." There are a lot of other things going on within the story that are more vital.

Audiences routinely confuse plot with plot device when it comes to movies. These devices can be big and obvious, or small and subtle.

Here are some examples of plot vs. plot device in popular action movies.

Die Hard

Plot: European terrorists seize control of a Los Angeles skyscraper, holding unsuspecting partygoers hostage. An off-duty cop is caught in the middle and tries to save his wife, and the day.

Plot Device(s): Christmas. In the movie we learn that the terrorists chose Christmas Eve as the best time for their assault because they knew the building would be mostly empty and vulnerable. Thus, they used the event of the executives' Christmas party as a way to gather hostages with minimal resistance. Christmas itself actually had little to do with the plot. (Yes, this is a way of saying that *Die Hard* is in fact, *not* a "Christmas movie.")

Predator

Plot: An elite Army Special Forces unit enters the Central American jungle on a rescue mission and is then stalked and hunted by a high-tech alien.

Plot Device: An Army helicopter carrying CIA personnel gets shot down and the operatives are taken hostage, prompting the Special Forces unit to attempt a rescue.

Rocky

Plot: A down-on-his-luck club fighter gets a million-to-one shot at the World Heavyweight title.

Plot Device: #1 contender Mac Lee Green breaks his hand, forcing Champion Apollo Creed to seek out a new opponent. Without the injury to Green, Rocky would never get his chance.

Independence Day

Plot: Advanced, powerful aliens attack earth's cities in an attempt to invade and dominate the planet.

Plot Device: 4th of July Weekend. The extraterrestrials had studied earth for years and believed the United States military may give them the most resistance, so they chose a nationally celebrated weekend to exploit as a vulnerability.

What we learn in those examples is how something – it could be an event, a date, or even an object – triggers the story to move forward. It doesn't mean it's what the movie is really about.

Because of that, we can understand how *Die Hard* isn't technically about Christmas. *Predator* isn't about a botched CIA operation. *Rocky* isn't the story of Mac Lee Green's untimely injury. *Independence Day* isn't about the 4th of July.

And *Field of Dreams*, as we'll see, isn't about baseball.

So, if baseball is only a plot device, how does it effectively move the story of *Field of Dreams*

174

along? If it's not exactly a "baseball movie" then what is it truly about? Well, it's about a lot of things. Let's take a deeper look.

If you build it...

In the film's opening scene, Ray Kinsella is out tending to his cornfield when he hears a voice – the famous line that people tend to *mis*quote to this day.

Almost immediately, he believes so strongly in what it *could* mean that he takes action virtually overnight. The Kinsellas were barely making a profit from their farm as it were, and to remove crucial acres of their main crop to build a seemingly useless baseball field would be financially suicidal. But Ray was a believer after all, and he just couldn't ignore the powerful force tugging at him to go forth with his crazy endeavor.

His loving wife Annie believed, too, almost without question.

Logic might dictate that she could have tried a little harder to talk Ray out of it (in the book she doesn't debate his plan at all), but she believed simply because Ray did.

Ironically, Ray actually took the message from the voice the wrong way. He thought the "he" in the "...he will come" line meant Shoeless Joe Jackson, when instead, the "he" meant his father. Even the mirage-like vision he had of Jackson on the field was a subtle hint to that end. More on that later.

Nevertheless, Ray made preparations to risk financial and possibly familial ruin to follow the voice, even unknowing of its true meaning. Annie, joining him on this big 'ol faith leap, tells Ray to go for it.

OK, but where does baseball fit in?

As Ray unfurls his farfetched plan, we see that each character is connected in some way through baseball. However, they also have their own unique paths that are all important, many of which have little or nothing to do with baseball at all.

As viewers of the film and readers of the novel, we sense an eldritch presence throughout the whole story. It is an unclear but unmistakable feeling that something out there is orchestrating all the events the characters experience. Many of these events are to the point that almost nothing is coincidental for them, individually or collectively.

Consider the following:

- We learn that Ray's destiny is to reconcile with his father. It isn't until the end of the film when he realizes that all of his prior adventures were leading him to that very point. In the process, while risking his own livelihood, he is able to help others find their way and create a little slice of heaven on earth for all people to experience and enjoy.

- Terence Mann's destiny (no, I don't believe he was actually dead the whole time as some theorists suggest), is to witness something so profound it will reignite his passion to write and influence others in the world again. His efforts, as it is later implied, will also serve as the perfect marketing plan for the field itself.

- Archibald "Moonlight" Graham got his lifelong wish to have a chance to bat in a big league game (or did he?). But more than that, he learned that his true destiny all along was to be a doctor. In realizing this, he set off crucial events that complete the whole tale.

- Shoeless Joe Jackson and his seven teammates, along with many other long-dead ballplayers got the chance to play ball again, this time presumably forever.

- Annie's brother Mark, the de-facto bad guy, is actually being practical out of love for his sister. Despite his apparent greed and disrespect for the farm, he really just wants to keep Annie's livelihood intact. His destiny, then, was to see through his corporate blinders and learn to believe in what's right, and what's possible.

The pattern here is evident: Only the ghostly ballplayers themselves might have their destinies actually be about playing baseball. For everyone else, it's everything but.

178

We can ascertain from this that baseball serves as the hub – it's what briefly brings the characters together before sending them off to what they are *really* supposed to do in life. Or in the afterlife in some cases.

In other words, baseball fits in only as a plot device.

Moonlight is the key

The truest, and most important depiction of manifest destiny at work in the film falls with Dr. Archibald "Moonlight" Graham. His storyline sets things in motion which further assert the movie is *not* about baseball.

When Ray visits Chisholm, Minnesota and inexplicably finds himself back in 1972 where he meets the aging Dr. Graham, the old doc reveals that his biggest wish was to get an at-bat in a big league game. He tells Ray how he longed to step into the batter's box on a sunny afternoon, wink mischievously at the pitcher, and then knock a triple. When Ray later picks up the ghost of a young

Graham hitchhiking his way through the Midwest, he believes he has an obvious way to grant Graham's wish: Just take him to his field and let him play in a game.

Things seem to fall into place as Graham plays in a game that very night, and hits a (metaphorical as we'll see) sacrifice fly. *Was that his only plate appearance?* There is no mention of what Graham did the rest of that game.

The next day, Graham is in the lineup again, but mid-game, he races off the field to rescue Ray's daughter Karin, who had fallen from the bleachers and was unconscious, choking on a hot dog. After saving her, Ray realizes that Graham cannot return to the field to keep playing. He had literally and symbolically crossed over into what he was truly supposed to be. We see Graham hesitate at the threshold to take that last step. Later he reassures a distraught Ray that it is perfectly alright that he can't return to the game. These actions strongly imply that, deep down, even in ghostly form, Graham knew his destiny all along was to be a doctor, not a baseball player.

Moonlight Graham's character, then, was all about sacrifice.

In life, he first sacrificed the continued pursuit of his baseball dream in order to become a doctor. In death, he sacrificed his second chance at playing ball to reacknowledge his true, medical calling.

Saving Karin allowed him to understand he did not belong at the field with the other ballplayers, so he left to join his wife, Alicia, in whatever afterlife that awaited them. But not before Shoeless Joe, in a touching moment, confirms to Graham that they accepted him as a ballplayer, too.

Thus, the *sacrifice* fly ball we see Graham hit was a nod to the sacrifices he had to make to stay on his destined path in life and even in death.

Sadly, it is not known if Moonlight Graham got to play a full game in his ghostly personage. If his sacrifice fly was his only plate appearance the night he arrived at the field (we were never shown the inning, so he could've been pinch hitting or was pulled before his next time up to bat), and if he crossed over to save Karin before batting the next day, then he still never technically got the *official* big league at-bat he wanted. He did have at least one plate appearance, though, which included his wink at the pitcher, so perhaps that was good enough for him.

Furthermore, Graham's penultimate departure sparked the final string of crucial events in the story.

"People will come, Ray..."

With Graham's selfless act of rescuing Karin, he helped fulfill *her* (at least immediate) destiny, which was to surprise everyone present with an idea on how to keep the field and her family's land.

Karin's plan, in turn, became the catalyst for Terence Mann to deliver his famous soliloquy. The captivating speech put Ray, by this point bankrupt, on the spot to make a decision: Sell the land to Mark and regain financial freedom but lose the field and its magic. Or take another leap of faith in the hopes of revealing everyone's lasting purpose. This was domino number two.

Ray made his mind up when he considered Karin's prophecy of people coming to the field and paying money to see proof of the hereafter. When Mann later reveals he will write about his firsthand experiences of the (baseball players' version anyway) afterlife, the perfect marketing plan falls into place.

In both instances, the world would have virtual proof of an existence beyond death. And for the Kinsellas, a seemingly endless stream of resources to maintain the land was on its way.

About those second chances...

There are many second chance opportunities for each character in the story: The eight White Sox players, and many others, get to play ball again; Moonlight Graham gets his plate appearance and sly wink at the pitcher; Terence Mann will return to writing and being a public figure; John Kinsella gets his shot at the big leagues and the opportunity to meet his daughter-in-law and granddaughter; and Ray gets a chance to make things right with – and fully unite – his family.

Throughout the movie, Ray hears three messages from an ethereal voice. He somewhat inaccurately assumes them to be about building the field for Shoeless Joe, taking Terence Mann to a game, and tracking down Moonlight Graham, in that order. While he was able to positively affect each person's fate, all three messages were also intended to be about his father, John, which Ray didn't realize at first.

Toward the end, when Mann is invited to go with the ghost players, it knocked down the third and final domino. This paved the way for Ray to finally get the chance he wished for, which brings the story full-circle.

When he put it all together, Ray assumed the voice was that of Shoeless Joe Jackson. But Jackson revealed, with a smile, that the voice was actually Ray's own. This shows that Jackson knew the endgame all along, and that he, the field, and baseball itself, were just parts of the journey to get Ray to that very moment.

Here we see our old friend, the plot device, beautifully doing its thing again.

Every character got their second chances and fulfilled destinies because baseball was the facilitator – but only insofar as to get people to where they needed to be.

Altogether it means that *Field of Dreams* is not really a baseball movie in the strictest sense.

The Japanese movie poster for *Field of Dreams* (posters in Japan are reportedly famous for revealing entire plots) nailed it, describing the movie as being about a farmer on a quest to meet with the ghost of his father. What each storyline and subplot in the movie boil down to, is really just about getting to *that* end point where Ray and his dad reconcile.

People will always consider it to be a baseball movie because, understandably, that's just the association they are used to.

But from technical and story standpoints, it does not fully qualify as such.

Nitpicking 101...to the Nth degree

OK, I just can't help this part. Pedantic though it may be, please indulge me here.

I'm usually the first one to say that in most films, you have to suspend your disbelief and just flow with it. Three decades later this movie wouldn't be so provocative and debatable if you didn't.

However, if *Field of Dreams* were a *true* baseball movie, it would be about a specific player, team, or season. Also, errors in some historical details may not have occurred:

- The real Archibald "Moonlight" Graham played his half-inning in 1905. In the movie it was 1922. A mostly insignificant detail, but just enough to irk any OCD baseball purist out there.
- Late in the movie we see what looks like some Philadelphia Athletics players on the field, judging by the logo on their jerseys.

They were 1920's style of uniforms, but with green lettering, sleeves, and socks. When the A's were in Philadelphia, with that uniform style, their colors were white and blue; they didn't change to green until after they moved to Kansas City in 1954. I suppose those could've been minor league or other non-MLB players on the field, but it's still worth noting for historical accuracy, and, OK, nitpicking. Yes, I know, it's fiction.

- One of the bigger goofs, aside from Ray Liotta's Shoeless Joe batting right handed, stems from the players knowing what year it is and being aware they are dead. In a prime screwup, Eddie Cicotte yells at Chick Gandil, citing a situation where, if he had hustled more, then Cicotte "would have won 20 games that year." Gandil, acknowledging they are in 1988, retorts "that was 68 years ago." This means the season the men were referring to was 1920. In that season, Cicotte actually won *21* games [2], and Gandil didn't even play because he had retired by then. This makes their little spat false on all levels.

- In the same argument, Gandil horribly mispronounces Eddie Cicotte's name as "Chi-coa-tee" instead of the correct "See-cott." [3] Perhaps that was an intentional dig between old teammates in the heat of an argument, but this inconsistency is worth noting.

If this was a movie intended to be squarely about baseball, then you might think little details like this would be smoothed out, more actual players mentioned, and more intricate scenes of the games themselves shown. These are the obvious criteria for sports movies.

Alas, while the theme of baseball is a common thread throughout the movie, there is a lot more

---

[2] https://www.baseball-reference.com/players/c/cicoted01.shtml

[3] https://www.baseball-reference.com/players/c/cicoted01.shtml

involved than just that. Let's also not forget that the movie is based on a wonderful novel, in which even more non-baseball elements and themes exist that did not make it to film.

Baseball in *Field of Dreams* is a prime mover in the story, for sure. But is it really a "baseball movie?"

No.

At least...not quite.

~ * ~

About the Author

Kevin Trusty is the author of *(Not) Just Another Ballgame*. He currently works as a freelance marketing copywriter, content producer and strategist, and blogger. Through the years he has worked with businesses of all sizes in virtually every industry on their marketing initiatives, content creation and strategy. He is a long time member of the *Society for American Baseball Research* (SABR) and maintains a blog on baseball history and other quirks of the game at radbournsrevenant.com. He has been published in dozens of newspapers, magazines, and websites, writing everything from advertorials and business profiles to event previews, historical features, and short fiction. His debut book, B*eyond Silence and Light,* a collection of short fiction, was published in September 2020.

His personal site/portfolio is at ktwriting.com. He resides in Joliet, Illinois.

About Gary Livacari

Baseball historian Gary Livacari is a longtime member of the *Society for American Baseball Research* (SABR) who enjoys writing about baseball. His forte is identifying ballplayers in old photographs, which led him to a role distinguishing and documenting players for baseball-fever.com. He also served as the editor for the Boston Public Library's *Leslie Jones Baseball Project*, in which he helped identify ballplayers in almost 3,000 photos from the 1930's and 1940's.

He has written two books, *Memorable World Series Moments*, and *Reflections on the 1919 Black Sox.* He has also authored biographies for SABR's ongoing *Bioproject*, as well as numerous articles and book reviews.

He is the co-editor of the *Old Time Baseball Photos* Facebook page, which currently has over 80,000 followers. He is also the developer, administrator, and editor of baseballhistorycomesalive.com.

Gary and his wife Nancy reside in Park Ridge, Illinois.

Contact him at Livac2@aol.com.

CREDITS

Kevin Trusty – Author

Denise M. Baran-Unland – Editor

Rebekah Baran – Production

Molly Errek – Cover Design

Gary Livacari – Foreword

Todd Calcaterra – Creative Assistant

RESEARCH SOURCES NOTED AND CONSULTED

Introduction

BleacherReport - NLDS Game 4: Umpire Jim Joyce Takes Bat out of Cardinals' Hands:
https://bit.ly/3wBhszq

Chapter 1

BleacherReport - Remembering the Washington Senators' 1924 World Series: https://bit.ly/3mvsEZU

1924 World Series Game 7 Box Score:
https://bit.ly/3rZ9QTC

Curly Ogden Wikipedia: https://bit.ly/3cV1kRA

Chapter 2

Cincinnati.com – "MLB's First Night Game Held at Crosley Field 85 Years Ago" by Jeff Suess:
https://bit.ly/3uwGaPz

Chicagology – Wrigley Field Lights Chronology:
https://bit.ly/39RiRbe

Baseball Hall of Fame - AAGPBL Shined a Light at Wrigley Field in 1943: https://bit.ly/3mu5y5z

SABR GamesProject – "July 1, 1943: All-American Girls Play First Game Under the Lights at Wrigley Field" by Merrie A. Fidler and Jim Nitz: https://bit.ly/2Q2abrx (article also appeared in "*Wrigley Field: The Friendly Confines at Clark and Addison*, (SABR 2019), edited by Gregory H. Wolf.)

AAGPBL League History: https://bit.ly/3wDiJpv

Box Score, July 1, 1943: https://bit.ly/3dB6e56

 (image originally from the Jul 2, 1943 edition of the Kenosha Evening News.)

AAGPBL Rules of Play: https://bit.ly/2PHyACZ

Chapter 3

Braves Field: Memorable Moments at Boston's Lost Diamond, Cecilia Tan and Bill Nowlin

1916 World Series Game 2 Box Score: https://bit.ly/3cY4ELz

Babe Ruth, Baseball Reference Page:
https://bit.ly/2Q5tFvi

1916 Boston Red Sox Statistics:
https://bit.ly/31WZWYa

Chapter 4

Jack Taylor, Baseball Reference Page:
https://bit.ly/3wAcDWV

Jack Taylor, Baseball Reference Bio:
https://bit.ly/3dKgwjw

Jack Taylor Wikipedia: https://bit.ly/3rZGeWe

Never Too Much Baseball – Jack Taylor's Complete
Game Streak: https://bit.ly/3rTtPU1

SABR BioProject on Jack Taylor by Daniel
Ginsburg: https://sabr.org/bioproj/person/jack-taylor-2/

Jack Taylor, Baseball Reference Page, 1906 season:
https://bit.ly/3wAMJCq

1907 World Series Summary: https://bit.ly/31X2yVY

Chapter 5

Crazy '08: How a Cast of Cranks, Rogues, Boneheads, and Magnates Created the Greatest Year in Baseball History, Cait Murphy

LA84 Foundation Digital Library Collection – Oct 17, 1908: https://bit.ly/3wziV9t

Baseball Almanac – Addie Joss' Perfect Game Box Score: https://bit.ly/3mq2jfJ

Addie Joss, Baseball Reference Page: https://bit.ly/3sYlBuV

Ed Walsh, Baseball Reference Page: https://bit.ly/39Ruv1I

MLB Career ERA Leaders: https://bit.ly/3fRfe8Y

MLB Career WHIP Leaders: https://bit.ly/2Q6a6TS

Chapter 6

Philadelphia Museum of Art - Centennial Origins: https://bit.ly/39TBCLn

SABR BioProject on Germany Schaefer by Dan Holmes: https://bit.ly/3wDAchR

The Glory of Their Times, Lawrence Ritter

Germany Schaefer Wikipedia:
https://bit.ly/2Q5yxR6

Germany Schaefer, Baseball Reference Page:
https://bit.ly/3sXsc8Y

Chapter 7

Smithsonian Magazine - "A Death at Home Plate" by Gilbert King: https://bit.ly/3sY9rm1

1921: The Yankees, The Giants, & the Battle for Baseball Supremacy In New York, Lyle Spatz and Steve Steinberg

Indians at Red Sox Box Score May 20, 1918:
https://bit.ly/3g3l5bJ

1918 Boston Red Sox Statistics:
https://bit.ly/3wDBBF9

1921 World Series Summary:
https://bit.ly/3mrYYwA

Carl Mays Wikipedia: https://bit.ly/2Rc2OhL

Chapter 8

SABR GamesProject - "May 5, 1917: On Second Thought, it's a No-Hitter for Ernie Koob": https://bit.ly/3s1lrlc

1917 Chicago White Sox Schedule: https://bit.ly/3rW49WQ

White Sox at Browns, May 5, 1917 Box Score: https://bit.ly/3cXG3qa

White Sox at Browns, May 6, 1917 Box Score: https://bit.ly/3dOziGK

Bob Groom, Baseball Reference Page: https://bit.ly/3fL1nBg

Joe Benz, Baseball Reference Page: https://bit.ly/3rZNrpg

Ernie Johnson, Baseball Reference Page: https://bit.ly/327Zw1v

1917 St. Louis Browns Schedule: https://bit.ly/3d2ytuN

Chapter 9

This Great Game – The 1917 Clean Sox:
https://bit.ly/3fPX2gf

Baseball History Comes Alive – "Heine Zimmerman Chases Eddie Collins Across the Plate in the 1917 World Series!": https://bit.ly/2RghqwJ

SABR BioProject on Heine Zimmerman by David Jones: https://bit.ly/3wA01iE

SABR BioProject on Bill Rariden by Charles F. Faber: https://bit.ly/3wAACFB

Simply Baseball Notebook – Heine Zimmerman:
https://bit.ly/3rYOKVN

1917 World Series Game 6 Box Score:
https://bit.ly/3sUHAmv

Chapter 10

Tris Speaker: The Rough and Tumble Life of a Baseball Legend, Timothy Gay

SABR GamesProject – "October 10, 1926: Pete Alexander Saves the Day": https://bit.ly/3utYXLo

SABR BioProject on Sport Sullivan by Bruce Allardice: https://bit.ly/3wDSEGO

CBS New York – "By the Numbers: Judging Babe Ruth's Attempted Steal in the 1926 World Series" by Father Gabe Costa: https://cbsloc.al/2Q5i27A

1928 Philadelphia Athletics Statistics: https://bit.ly/3sYzqJZ

Baseball Egg – "Babe Ruth's Failed Stolen Base Attempt Ended the 1926 World Series, Or Did It?" by Dan Holmes: https://bit.ly/3rWN8M3

1926 World Series Game 7 Box Score: https://bit.ly/3wLKDzY

Chapter 11

Ghosts of DC – "The Time Walter Johnson Pitched 18 Innings in One Game!": https://bit.ly/3rY4M23

Library of Congress – *Washington Herald*, May 16, 1918, P. 12: https://bit.ly/2RkbhzL

White Sox at Senators May 15, 1918 Box Score: https://bit.ly/3fPDNTS

SABR BioProject on Lefty Williams by Jacob Pomrenke: https://bit.ly/3fRcf0w

Chapter 12

1919 Cincinnati Reds Statistics: https://bit.ly/3mu7gUL

1919 Chicago White Sox Statistics: https://bit.ly/3rW3a8P

The 1919 Reds: Requiem for the Robbed by Jeff Kallman in SABR's *Black Sox Scandal Research Committee Newsletter vol 10 No. 2, December 2018*

SABR BioProject on Red Faber by Brian Cooper: https://bit.ly/2Q00tWG

SABR BioProject on Eddie Cicotte by Jim Sandoval: https://bit.ly/3uzsiUv

Chapter 13

Baseball Hall of Fame – "Mathewson Throws Third Shutout in Series to Take Title" by Bridget Bielefeld: https://bit.ly/2R7T348

1905 World Series Summary: https://bit.ly/3a91mnd

Archibald "Moonlight" Graham, Baseball Reference Page: https://bit.ly/3sZEzBy

Joe McGinnity, Baseball Reference Page: https://bit.ly/3uzsTWi

Chapter 14

2016 World Series Game 7 Box Score: https://bit.ly/39PVS0r

DnaInfo – "5 Million People Attend Cubs Rally and Parade, City Estimates" by Heather Cherone: https://bit.ly/3t0O1o7

Chapter 15

Shoeless Joe, W.P. Kinsella

Eight Men Out, Eliot Asinof

Eight Men Out movie

Field of Dreams movie

Eddie Cicotte, Baseball Reference Page: https://bit.ly/2PHMncJ

SABR – "Eight Myths Out: Appendix of Errors in 'Eight Men Out' Book and Film" by Bill Lamb: https://bit.ly/31U7DhR